RESEARCH FOUNDATION REVIEW 2015

CFA Institute
Research
Foundation

Statement of Purpose

The CFA Institute Research Foundation is a not-for-profit organization established to promote the development and dissemination of relevant research for investment practitioners worldwide.

ISBN 978-1-934667-97-2

February 2016

CONTENTS

I. THE YEAR IN REVIEW

II. MONOGRAPH SUMMARIES

III. LITERATURE REVIEW SUMMARIES

IV. RF BRIEFS SUMMARIES

V. MULTIMEDIA SUMMARIES

VI. WORKSHOP FOR THE PRACTITIONER SUMMARIES

VII. 50TH ANNIVERSARY FORUM

VIII. AWARDS AND RECOGNITION

IX. PAST AND FUTURE PUBLICATIONS

I. THE YEAR IN REVIEW

WHY RESEARCH IS SO IMPORTANT: A MESSAGE FROM PAUL SMITH, CFA

Paul Smith, CFA
President and CEO
CFA Institute

We live in an information age, but because not everything we read is true, we must validate. And the best way to validate information is through research. As a result, finding a reliable source is critical; it allows you to gain important knowledge that helps you make decisions in business and also in life. This knowledge, in turn, helps to build your own credibility and reputation. When you find the answers, research helps you prove your point. And when you cannot find the answers, new opportunities emerge. It is these opportunities that are at the core of the CFA Institute Research Foundation.

Over the past 50 years, the investment management profession has dramatically evolved from a dispersed group of statisticians to a global profession of investment practitioners with a highly respected credential. We have come out of the back room and into the board room. This change would not have happened without the efforts of early pioneers who saw the need for critical research that informed those of us who work in and lead the profession.

Through the decades, the Research Foundation has filled a void. When the Institute of Chartered Financial Analysts (ICFA) Executive Director C. Stewart Sheppard launched the Research Foundation in 1965, the CFA Program curriculum was sadly lacking in materials, and the Research Foundation (RF) stepped in to fill that void.

Back then, there were few sources of original research, so the RF sponsored new research. In the 1960s, publishing textbooks was important but so was sponsoring original monographs, seminars, and papers on topics not well covered in the existing literature. The RF filled this vacuum, developing offerings that also fulfilled one of the founding purposes of the ICFA: to guide and encourage the continuing education of persons engaged in the professional practice of financial analysis.

Throughout the years, numerous people have contributed to the financial support of the RF, particularly those dedicated to the cause of fostering independent research for investment practitioners. Key leaders like Pete Morley, CFA, Gene Sit, CFA, George Noyes, CFA, and Fred Speece, Jr., CFA, worked tirelessly to raise an endowment. Gary Brinson, CFA, made a generous gift that was particularly important in that effort. Many authors voluntarily donated the royalties from their books to the RF. We are, and forever will be, in their debt.

Today, the purpose of the RF is to sponsor, publish, and distribute cutting-edge research on topics that contribute to or improve global investment practices and the CFA Institute Global Body of Investment Knowledge, which is used by investment professionals all over the world. The RF also delivers research through in-person conferences and online webinars, and it recognizes excellence in contributions to the global investment community through the James R. Vertin Award. Research produced by the RF has been widely quoted, sometimes for many years because much of the information presented has been way ahead of its time.

Congratulations on 50 years of excellence in research, and I look forward to the next 50! We are all better investment professionals because of the efforts of the many volunteers who have been so passionate about finding the answers.

MESSAGE FROM THE RESEARCH FOUNDATION CHAIR

John T. Grier, CFA
Chair
The CFA Institute Research Foundation

As chair of the CFA Institute Research Foundation Board of Trustees, I invite you to join me in celebrating our 50th anniversary and in extending a sincere thank you to everyone who has contributed to our success. The Research Foundation has a straightforward yet broad and bold mission: to provide independent, high-quality research that helps investment professionals effectively fulfill their duties with prudence, loyalty, and care.

The Research Foundation was established in 1965 and endowed by generous contributions from a number of prominent investment professionals and organizations. We are governed by an all-volunteer board of trustees; are supported by a small, loyal staff; and receive exceptional production assistance from CFA Institute. However, it is the support of engaged readers like you and the thorough work of our talented authors that ultimately defines our success. This consistent and strong backing from all stakeholders has enabled the Research Foundation to advance the understanding of investment markets and helped position us to keep pace with today's rapidly changing environment.

Over the decades, our audience has evolved from a small society of US security analysts to a worldwide community that reflects the diversity of the modern investment industry—security analysts, portfolio managers, traders, brokers, consultants, asset owners, regulators, and academics. To address the needs of such a broad audience, the Research Foundation engages practitioner and academic authors who are committed to producing independent investment research that is oriented to the practical application of investment finance. The research topics cover all fields relevant to investment professionals, and although that coverage may involve topical investment issues, our research is meant to distinguish itself not by its timeliness but rather by its timelessness.

The majority of our research is published in book form, but we also produce literature reviews, webinars, workshops, audiobooks, and starting this year, shorter research pieces called "RF Briefs." All Research Foundation materials are distributed online for free and are available in hardcopy format for a nominal charge. We strive to produce the highest quality research that is distributed in ways that are easy to consume so that we can better serve you, our growing and increasingly diverse readership.

Photo credit: Alan Barnett.

Research Foundation content through the decades.

I hope you enjoy this year's edition of the *Research Foundation Review*, and I encourage you to browse our extensive research library, which is hosted on the CFA Institute website and available on such other platforms as Kindle, iBook, SSRN, and Savvy Investor. In closing, I invite you to attend one of the Research Foundation Annual Workshops that are held the opening day of each CFA Institute Annual Conference. The workshops provide an excellent opportunity to dive deeper into important investment topics and to vigorously discuss research with your peers.

EXECUTIVE DIRECTOR'S REPORT

Bud Haslett, CFA
Executive Director
The CFA Institute Research Foundation

Welcome to the 50th anniversary edition of the *Research Foundation Review*. Since 1965, the CFA Institute Research Foundation (RF) has published relevant, high-quality content for the investment practitioner. We are looking forward to continuing our mission for the next 50 years and beyond and hope you can continue to join us for the journey.

Research Foundation content had another strong year in 2015 with the publication of insightful books on geopolitics, exchange-traded funds, trading and electronic markets, and the global asset management business. In addition, a literature review on longevity risk and retirement income was also produced. Spending a few minutes reading the summaries of these works will enhance your knowledge as an investment professional. And by taking the extra effort to read the complete content for those books most relevant to you, your knowledge can be expanded even further.

In addition to our usual RF content offerings of books and literature reviews, we are pleased to announce a new product, RF Briefs. The Briefs feature more concise content for the busy, on-the-go investment professional. Although short to read, the Briefs are long on insights. Our first Brief on risk profiling is listed in this review, with future Briefs on annuities, behavioral finance, structured products, and financial technology coming out in 2016 and beyond. To help support the Briefs, the RF has created Regional Research Councils in the Americas, APAC (Asia Pacific), and EMEA (Europe, Middle East, and Africa) to source more topics and authors of a global and regional nature.

The multimedia offerings for 2015 include an audiobook version of last year's smash hit *Investment Management: A Science to Teach or an Art to Learn?* The audiobook gives you a chance to enjoy RF content in your car, on a plane, or anywhere you can pop on your headphones and listen. An enlightening video presentation by Brian Singer, CFA, on portfolio diversification is also available for your viewing pleasure. Additional video content is featured in other sections of the review.

The Research Foundation's 14th Annual Workshop for the Practitioner, held at the CFA Institute Annual Conference in Frankfurt, Germany, featured RF authors Pippa Malmgren and Joachim Klement, CFA, as esteemed speakers. Both discussed their RF content during the workshop's free session available to all attendees of the annual conference. We look forward to welcoming Larry Harris, CFA, and Keith Ambachtsheer as speakers for the 15th annual workshop, which will be held in Montréal in May 2016.

The New York Society of Security Analysts (NYSSA) hosted celebrations for the RF 50th anniversary, and a sold-out crowd of almost 200 were treated to panel discussions titled "Evolution of Investment Research" and "Helping the Investment Profession." Moderators Larry Siegel and Jason Zweig led the forums with panelists Stephen J. Brown, Jason Hsu, Joachim Klement, CFA, Ted Aronson, CFA, Vikram Kuriyan, CFA, Fred Lebel, CFA, and Paul Smith, CFA, providing insights. Video for both forums is available as is a rousing acceptance speech by Vertin Award winner Frank Fabozzi, CFA, whose comments followed the panels.

Fabozzi joins a distinguished list of previous Vertin Award winners, including William Sharpe, Robert Shiller, Peter Bernstein, Andrew Lo, and others who have been recognized for their lifetime contributions to investment research. We are delighted to include Fabozzi among these legendary authors and especially thank him for sharing his fixed-income content with legions of current and former CFA Program candidates (including myself, way back in the 1990s) as part of the CFA Program exam material.

CFA Institute member societies play an important role in Research Foundation activities, and we continue to grant those who do it the best the RF Society Award. In 2015, we proudly added seven societies to the growing list of award winners. The RF thanks all societies for participating in RF-related activities and hopes that 2016 is the year when we reach our goal of 100% society participation. A special thanks goes out to the societies that have hosted, and will be hosting, the Research Foundation board meetings. Your tremendous efforts to make our board meetings and events successful are truly appreciated.

Recently, the RF and the Standards and Advocacy group of CFA Institute (led by Managing Director Kurt Schacht, CFA) became partners in driving the vision of the future for investment management practitioners. To showcase the excellent content published by the entire group, we are delighted to include in this review a listing and links to various of the group's publications, including content from the Future of Finance team. We are excited to be working with the entire group to achieve our shared goal.

Looking ahead to 2016, the RF has many great offerings in the works, including a financial market history book and video. This content is based on an RF-supported event at the Cambridge University Judge School of Business coordinated by David Chambers and Elroy Dimson. We have included a summary of this content in this review and hope you will look forward to reading the full book in the near future.

Serving as executive director of the Research Foundation continues to be the greatest honor of my professional career. The position is part labor of love, part exhilarating challenge, and part satisfying accomplishment, with a (fortunately) very small dash of the inevitable frustration that comes along with operating any not-for-profit organization such as ours. But through it all, with the help of the amazing CFA Institute leadership and staff, the engaged RF board members, talented authors, and thousands of donors like you, the hidden gem of CFA Institute is no longer so hidden. On this 50th anniversary of the Research Foundation, we sincerely thank you all and pledge our diligence in continuing to make the RF great.

RESEARCH DIRECTOR'S REPORT

Laurence B. Siegel
Gary P. Brinson Director of Research
The CFA Institute Research Foundation

In 2015, the CFA Institute Research Foundation published four research monographs and a literature review. We also introduced an exciting new research outlet, RF Briefs, which are global in origin.

Monographs

Pippa Malmgren, *Geopolitics for Investors*

Pippa Malmgren's March 2015 monograph introduces readers to the basic concepts of geopolitics and describes its influence on investment risk and performance. Malmgren, a policy analyst, investment manager, and public speaker, was special assistant to the president for economic policy during the George W. Bush administration.

Malmgren provides this definition: "Geopolitics generally refers to a state's projection of power abroad by any means or tools of statecraft." The present is a stressful time in geopolitics, and investors are affected more than usually by the projection of power on the part of various state and nonstate actors. The wild fluctuations in oil prices are a case in point.

To help geopolitics come to life, Malmgren draws some terminology from academic geography. An *ecumene*, for example, is the most economically significant part of a region. London is one. It is supported agriculturally by the rest of the United Kingdom and, in turn, supports the rest fiscally. Thus, there is a natural tension between London and its hinterlands. Malmgren also emphasizes the use of names (such as Vladimir Putin's Novorossiya, "New Russia," to make expansionist claims) and maps (China's nine-dash map of the South China Sea, constructed for similar purposes).

Turning to practical applications of geopolitics for investors, Malmgren notes that investors are in unfamiliar territory when dealing with intercountry stresses and conflicts. In times of geopolitical trouble, investors turn to "experts," who may or may not have valuable knowledge. Malmgren notes, "Few fund managers would consider a couple of phone calls with an 'expert' on a company proper due diligence for making an equity investment in that company. But they will take that approach when it comes to geopolitics." She sets forth a number of strategies for dealing with this knowledge deficit in an asset management context.

A number of helpful cartograms (maps drawn other than in proportion to geographical area) show the distribution of world population, GDP, water and food resources, and military expenditures. These maps help readers visualize the geopolitical trends and troubles discussed by the author.

Joanne M. Hill, Dave Nadig, and Matt Hougan, *A Comprehensive Guide to Exchange-Traded Funds (ETFs)*

In an encyclopedic May 2015 research monograph, Joanne Hill, Dave Nadig, and Matt Hougan—all deeply involved in the founding of the exchange-traded fund (ETF) industry—describe the ETF "ecosystem" that has developed since these funds came to prominence about two decades ago. ETFs, which are portfolios (usually index funds) of stocks or other assets, enable investors to trade portfolios of stocks as they would individual stocks but trade continuously on an exchange instead of at the end of each day as a traditional mutual fund trades. The issuance of ETFs thus democratizes and expands on the program trading (portfolio trading) techniques used on Wall Street before ETFs emerged and allows many different kinds of risk to be taken or hedged.

Since ETFs were first issued, an astonishing array of portfolios has been put on the ETF platform, and as the authors write, "At the end of September 2014, 5,463 ETFs and ETPs [exchange-traded products], with . . . assets of $2.63 trillion from 225 providers were listed on 61 exchanges in 49 countries."

Hill et al. describe the complex creation and redemption processes for ETFs and explain how "authorized participants" (typically, broker/dealers) make a market in these funds and keep their prices closely aligned with the prices of the underlying securities.

A major section covers the regulatory structure under which ETFs operate. This information is important because ETFs are partly a portfolio, partly a security, and in some cases, partly a derivative. The authors then evaluate the efficiency of ETFs in "closely track[ing] the indexes on which they are based and charge[ing] low and predictable investment costs." Such efficiency is valuable because low fees and other costs, which are one of the primary attractions of index funds, should also be characteristic of index ETFs. The authors also consider the trading efficiency of ETFs; that is, the investor should be able to manage trading costs to a low level even though "ETFs [are] used extensively for tactical trading," not only long-term investing. In the portfolio management section, the authors show how ETFs can be used to achieve a variety of risk exposures and hedges, in both the short run and the long run.

The authors then review the ETF markets in each major asset class, including equities, fixed income, commodities, currencies, and alternative investments. Finally, they discuss the use of leveraged and inverse ETFs, which are controversial because many investors misunderstand how these funds will perform if held for the long run.

An appendix on international ETFs by Deborah Fuhr rounds out the book and provides basic historical and current information on particular ETFs in all the major countries in which they trade.

Larry Harris, CFA, *Trading and Electronic Markets: What Investment Professionals Need to Know*

Few institutions or practices have changed as quickly in recent years as equity trading. Not that long ago, trading was a person-to-person affair conducted by specialists on the exchange floor and dealers in the OTC market; now, trading is almost entirely electronic. High-frequency traders, who do not hold any long-term investment positions, make up a large share of volume. It is a new world, requiring re-education of everyone who learned about trading before this century.

Larry Harris, the former chief economist of the US Securities and Exchange Commission and a University of Southern California finance professor, fills the need for re-education with his October 2015 book *Trading and Electronic Markets*. Harris begins by setting forth a taxonomy of traders grouped by why they trade. "Value and news" traders have information that could help them beat the market. "Parasitic" traders try to make money off knowledge about who else is trading. "Utilitarian" traders buy to move money from the present to the future or sell to raise money they need now. "Dealers" make money by providing liquidity to other traders. Harris reminds the reader that, because active management is a zero-sum game relative to a properly selected benchmark, not all traders can make money. Some make money at the expense of others.

Harris then addresses the measurement of trading costs. Trading is a surprisingly large contributor to the cost of investing. By managing these costs, investors can improve their performance by meaningful amounts.

Electronic trading is the focus of a major section of the book. Harris explains how it works and delineates the roles of computers and of people. He considers the desirability of speed and the cost savings provided by this new way of doing business. Harris then addresses nine "practitioner and regulatory issues associated with fast electronic markets." Among them is the accusation that the "arms race" among high-frequency traders raises costs rather than lowering them as some claim. Harris also explains new practices such as "dark pools" and "maker–taker" pricing. He concludes with an appendix that describes, and attempts to explain, the "flash crash" that trimmed 5% off the market indexes in a short period on 6 May 2010 and was followed by a quick recovery.

Ingo Walter, *The Industrial Organization of the Global Asset Management Business*

In his December 2015 book, Ingo Walter, a dean and professor of finance, corporate governance, and ethics at New York University's Stern School of Business, presents an "industrial organization" approach to understanding investment management as a business. Industrial organization traditionally applies to the structure (e.g., relative size), conduct (e.g., monopolist versus competitor), and performance (e.g., profitability) of companies in an industry. Although Walter does not follow this outline exactly, it is the inspiration for his work. By turning the research lens around and looking at ourselves—that is, investment managers—instead of the financial markets, Walter produces a survey of the institutional layout of our business that is especially valuable to students, CFA Program candidates and CFA charterholders, and rising professionals.

Walter begins by examining the worldwide stock of financial assets, which totals $212 trillion, or about $30,000 for every man, woman, and child on earth. Of this vast fortune, a large majority is in fixed-income assets and deposit instruments. Equities make up "only" $54 trillion. (These data are 2010 figures; current numbers are larger because of the bull market.)

The distribution of world wealth can be understood along several dimensions: by asset class, by country, by who manages it, and so forth. After briefly considering the first two dimensions, Walter shows how this wealth is apportioned among its various stewards: pension funds, mutual funds, alternatives managers, and private wealth managers. (Some other categories, such as insurance reserves, sovereign wealth funds, and central bank reserves, are considered only in passing.) Walter details the risks, regulatory and cultural challenges, and business opportunities facing each category of steward. As he delineates these factors, he maintains a global perspective, which is badly needed at this time when home-country bias is still a major barrier to business progress and investment understanding.

Walter concludes by asking whether asset management firms pose systemic risks. Because most asset management firms own essentially no assets, doing their work as agents for others (asset owners), Walter concludes that the answer is generally no. The use of leverage and derivatives, however, and the crossover in certain firms between asset management and businesses such as investment banking allow asset managers to become implicated in systemic risk in certain circumstances.

Literature Reviews

Patrick J. Collins, CFA, Huy D. Lam, CFA, and Josh Stampfli, *Longevity Risk and Retirement Income Planning*

In this review, Patrick Collins, a wealth adviser and adjunct professor in the School of Management at the University of San Francisco, teams up with his colleague Huy Lam and trader Josh Stampfli to review the extensive literature on longevity risk, portfolio "decumulation," and other issues surrounding the spending of assets out of a portfolio over an individual's lifetime. (Spending rules for institutions are not covered.) The authors emphasize "sustainability," by which they mean the ability of a portfolio to withstand a given stream of withdrawals without becoming depleted.

Spending out of an investment portfolio involves three key variables: return, longevity (the amount of time the money needs to last), and volatility. Volatility is crucial because spending out of a volatile portfolio can be more damaging to portfolio sustainability than spending out of a stable one; yet, investors seek volatility in order to earn a return premium, which is likely but not guaranteed. This tension pervades all decisions about spending rules.

The review is organized into two major sections. The first covers the risk management literature produced in 1965–2005 as it applies to individual investors. The authors bring the insurance and annuities literature, as well as mainstream finance literature, to bear on issues in life-cycle finance. This approach is particularly welcome because the pioneering 1965 work of Menahem Yaari on annuities spawned a literature that is often overlooked by mainstream finance academics and practitioners.

The second section covers recent (2005–14) innovations. The literature has moved from an emphasis on "fixed asset allocations and bright-line spending rules" to "dynamic risk monitoring." The authors devote considerable space to one specific model, set forth in 2012 by former University of California Berkeley Finance Professor Gordon Pye in his book *The Retrenchment Rule*. Pye argues that investors can spend more than the traditional 4% of at-retirement capital if they are willing to cut spending later in retirement. He explains how to engineer a spending glide path such that consumption is satisfactory over the entire in-retirement period.

As investors struggle with the many sources of conflicting advice on how to invest for retirement and then spend the accumulated savings, the literature reviewed by Collins, Lam, and Stampfli will become increasingly important.

RF Briefs

In our first offering in this category, *Investor Risk Profiling: An Overview,* Joachim Klement, CFA, a private wealth adviser and vice chair of the CFA Institute Research Foundation, discusses the task of assessing an investor's risk tolerance. His thesis is that the psychological questionnaires often used to assess risk tolerance are unreliable and that better methods exist. Among these methods are (1) a self-reported financial behavior history analogous to the medical history obtained from patients by doctors and (2) a record of the investor's past financial transactions. One reason for the unreliability of psychological questionnaires is that, although investors may know how they would behave when the stakes are low (such as when betting a small sum of money), they do not know and cannot tell the investigator how they would behave when their life savings are at stake. Thus, the adviser obtains little information about the investor's true risk preferences from a questionnaire and would benefit from using the alternative methods that Klement recommends.

II. MONOGRAPH SUMMARIES

GEOPOLITICS FOR INVESTORS (A SUMMARY)

by Pippa Malmgren
Summary prepared by Pippa Malmgren

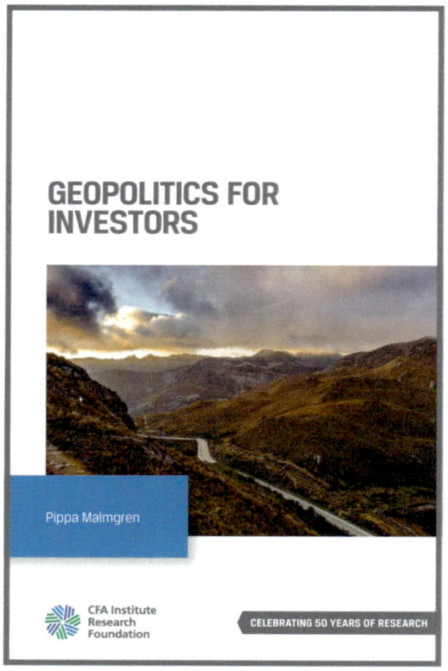

The CFA Institute Research Foundation presents *Geopolitics for Investors* to help investors manage the "new geopolitics" that is now influencing the investment landscape. The book focuses on how to think about geopolitics so that investors can better determine what they think about geopolitics and its impact on markets and prices.

It is written for a generation that has known only a post–Cold War world. Some 25 years ago, the Berlin Wall fell and the world economy benefitted from the resulting "great moderation of inflation" and "peace dividend." The introduction of billions of new workers into the world economy drove wages and prices down and GDP up. It also drove geopolitics off the landscape, largely because, with so much growth, everyone's needs could be met. That left less to argue about. Now, 25 years later, we find the world descending again into contentious geopolitics. We hear fiery, provocative language between the world's superpowers. We see very near misses between Russian fighter jets and US spy planes and between US and Chinese naval vessels. Air incursions and disputes over borders and territory are becoming commonplace. Social unrest is percolating in many parts of the world. Non-state actors, ranging from separatists in Ukraine to ISIL, are changing the landscape of risk. Established borders, such as the Sykes–Picot borders in the Middle East and the US–Mexican border, are disintegrating before our eyes. These developments all have market implications that investors need to consider.

The current generation of fund managers and investors has known only a world in which geopolitics has been relatively subdued compared with the Cold War period. From an investor's perspective, the wars in Afghanistan, Iraq, and Syria have been reasonably localised events, with relatively limited market consequences. The bigger question now is whether investors are safe to assume that the United States, Russia, and China will always find more benefit in cooperation than in conflict. Is this assumption still true? China and Russia are not only challenging the United States from a strategic perspective. They—and many others—are also challenging the US dollar's role as the reserve currency. The US philosophy that has underpinned the postwar world economic architecture is increasingly questioned. Long-standing relationships—including the alignments between Saudi Arabia and the United States, between Britain and the EU, and between the EU and the United States—are also changing because of geopolitics and can no longer be taken for granted. Internal alignments are changing as well.

The return of geopolitics to the landscape has investment implications. Although it is easy to assume that social unrest, conflict, and other forms of geopolitics render the landscape "uninvestable," such events also create opportunities. Tunisia—where the Arab Spring started—launched a record number of IPOs, all successful, only one year after that event in spite of (or perhaps because of) a radical change in governance. Markets adjusted during the height of the "mutual assured destruction" days of the Cold War. Geopolitical tensions do not preclude good investment performance. But ignorance of geopolitics can undermine performance.

The complete book can be found at www.cfapubs.org/toc/rf/2015/2015/1.

Use your mobile device to scan the QR code to go straight to the webpage.

A COMPREHENSIVE GUIDE TO EXCHANGE-TRADED FUNDS (ETFs) (A SUMMARY)

by Joanne M. Hill, Dave Nadig, and Matt Hougan, with an appendix on international ETFs by Deborah Fuhr
Summary prepared by Joanne M. Hill, Dave Nadig, and Matt Hougan

The purpose of our book is to help investors understand and effectively use exchange-traded funds (ETFs) to meet their investment return and risk objectives.[1] Introduced just over 25 years ago, ETFs are now one of the fastest-growing segments of the investment management business. The book covers the details of how ETFs work, their unique investment and trading features, their regulatory structure, the history of the product structure, and the evolution of ETFs across asset classes and into active investment products. It also covers how they fit into the portfolio management process and how best to evaluate ETFs to identify the right funds to fit any particular investment or trading objective. Separate chapters provide insights into ETFs by asset class and category, including equity, fixed-income, commodity, currency, alternative, and leveraged and inverse ETFs.

A special appendix by Deborah Fuhr, managing partner of ETFGI, details the global footprint of ETFs—covering the distribution of assets by country and region from Australia to Latin America. This section captures the differentiating features of exchange-traded products around the globe; it highlights the primary issuers, asset class breakdown, and structures, along with the size of ETF assets relative to mutual funds and institutional versus retail participation.

[1]Throughout the book, we use "ETF" as a generic acronym for a range of exchange-traded products, including those organized under the Investment Company Act of 1940, various trust structures, and exchange-traded notes.

The Basics

At their core, ETFs are hybrid investment products, with many of the investment features of mutual funds married to the trading features of common stocks. Like in a mutual fund, an investor buys shares in an ETF to own a proportional interest in the pooled assets, which are generally managed by an investment adviser for a fee. But unlike mutual fund shares, ETF shares are traded in continuous markets on global stock exchanges, can be bought and sold through brokerage accounts, and have continuous pricing and liquidity throughout the trading day. Thus, they can be margined, lent, shorted, or subjected to any other strategy used by sophisticated equity investors.

In early 2015, the assets of exchange-traded funds and notes globally were $2.9 trillion according to ETFGI, with $2 trillion in the United States. That amount represents over 5,000 individual ETFs from 247 providers listed on 63 exchanges in 51 different countries.[2] In 2013, ETFs represented more than 11% of all mutual fund assets, up from 2% a decade earlier, and they have continued to attract both individual and institutional investor assets. Even more impressive is that on any given day, ETFs typically represent between 25% and 40% of the total dollar volume traded on US exchanges. In short, in just over two decades, these innovative financial products have gone from an afterthought to one of the most important forces shaping how investors invest and how the market itself functions. The outlook for continued growth is strong; now virtually all large asset managers (including such mutual fund giants as PIMCO, Fidelity, and JP Morgan Investment Management) are moving aggressively into the ETF space.

Benefits of Using ETFs as Investment Vehicles

The starting point to understanding the value proposition of ETFs is consideration of the features of ETFs that have made these funds so successful. First and foremost is the *cost savings of index strategies*. Most ETFs are index funds and, therefore, do not bear the costs of discretionary, active portfolio management, but another part of the cost advantage is implied by their name: The funds are *exchange traded*. The costs of recording who the buyer or seller is, sending him or her prospectus documents, handling inquiries, and other factors are all borne by the broker. ETFs are generally cheaper to run and distribute than traditional mutual funds, active institutional strategies, and certainly hedge funds. Thus, ETFs are generally cheaper to own.

A second core benefit of ETFs is simply *access*. ETFs have created a wealth of new portfolio construction opportunities for a broad range of investors, regardless of the size of their investment holdings or horizon, by opening up new asset classes for investing.

---

[2]ETFGI Press Release (9 April 2015): etfgi.com.

Prior to the growth of ETFs, owning such assets as gold bullion, emerging market bonds, currencies, volatility, or alternative assets was difficult and costly except for large institutional investors. ETFs have made all areas of the capital markets accessible for any investor with a brokerage account. In addition, ETFs can be sold short and, in some cases, have inverse exposure as an investment objective; this feature makes access possible for those seeking to profit from decreases as well as increases in price.

Because ETFs trade like equities, they have democratized the investment process, offering *liquidity* and providing a marketplace where all types of investors, regardless of asset size or length of time horizon, can come together and transact in a transparent manner with the regulatory protections of exchange-traded stocks and, in most cases, registered investment companies.

Transparency is another key benefit because most ETF providers display their entire portfolios on a daily basis through their websites, and this information is also picked up by financial data services.

Another key benefit of ETFs to investors is *tax efficiency*. In most situations, ETFs have a marked advantage over mutual funds when it comes to after-tax returns. There are two reasons for greater tax efficiency with ETFs: lower portfolio turnover and the ability to do in-kind redemptions, which keeps capital gain (and loss) distributions low in contrast to mutual funds. In 2013, according to the Investment Company Institute, fully 51% of all equity mutual fund share classes paid out capital gains. Only 3.87% of ETFs did. And of that 3.87%, a tiny fraction—only seven funds—paid out gains that were significant (more than 2% of net asset value).

Drawbacks in Utilizing ETFs for Investing

ETFs have numerous benefits, but investors should be aware of a number of potential drawbacks. Investors new to ETFs and their sometimes-novel asset classes and strategies may be unfamiliar with the underlying assets, drivers of return, and associated risks. Even an investor who is well versed in the international equity market may not be familiar with the inherent risks of, say, international corporate bonds, direct currency investing, or emerging market small-capitalization stocks. Those exposures have not been offered in a mutual fund package with any regularity, but they are significant and regular features of the ETF landscape.

Furthermore, many alternative ETFs—funds providing exposure through futures, notes, or swaps—involve portfolio structures, counterparty risks, and unfamiliar tax treatments, not because of the nature of the underlying exposures but because of the means of accessing them. ETFs offering exposure to commodities, leveraged and inverse returns, currency, or volatility are particularly subject to this caution. Investors considering the less-conventional investment strategies may need to dive deeper into the features of the strategies than they would when investing with stocks and bonds, which are more straightforward investments. Education is the key to understanding the various risks in certain asset classes and strategies.

Although ETFs have lower expense ratios than mutual funds, some costs must be considered that could differ from those associated with mutual funds. With exchange tradability comes the burden of paying commissions, bid–ask spreads, and, potentially, premiums and discounts to net asset value. As with trading stocks, these costs can affect returns. In the case of an institutional mutual fund, the fund incurs the costs of buying and selling the underlying securities with each day's cash flow or changes in portfolio holdings. The trading costs of commissions and market impact show up in fund performance but are otherwise largely hidden from the mutual fund investor.

ETF Strategies in Portfolio Management

Tactical strategies incorporating ETFs were among the first uses for ETFs and continue to be the most common way in which investors use ETFs. Investing excess cash (often from dividends or new investment) with ETFs allows these institutional investors to stay fully invested quickly and cheaply. In addition, many institutional investors have dedicated tactical pools to respond to short-term market conditions. Much of this tactical trading is now done with ETFs because of their low cost, liquidity, and breadth of offerings. Also, registered investment advisers and financial advisers now typically have an allocation for their client portfolios that uses ETFs for opportunistic investing. A growing category of ETF managers, now tracked by Morningstar, devote 50% or more of their portfolios to ETFs and earn fees by offering tactical and strategic allocation across the various asset classes, either as wealth managers or as part of institutional mandates.

But ETFs are becoming increasingly popular for long-term holdings as well. In fact, many asset owners (such as pension funds, endowments, and foundations) are increasingly using ETFs for strategic asset allocation and as strategy tools within asset classes. Another long-term strategic application of ETFs is to use a "strategy index" ETF or actively managed ETF within an asset class, replacing a more traditional mutual fund or separate account option—after considering the relative performance, risk profile, fees, transparency, and liquidity of the ETF versus competitors. The choices here are expanding as ETF managers work with index providers to design innovative rules-based strategies, some of which have been labeled "smart beta," that are usually quantitative rules packaged in an ETF wrapper. In addition, many mutual fund managers have been following the lead of PIMCO and have begun offering ETF versions of their most popular mutual fund products.

Thematic or style tilting is another strategy that is increasingly implemented with ETFs for both short- and long-term investment horizons. These themes may include strategies based on fundamental or dividend-based stock weighting, quantitative stock selection factors, low-volatility stocks, or even stocks of companies doing buybacks or achieving dividend growth. Fixed-income indexes have also been constructed around securities from debt issuers with high yields or with hedged duration exposures. International investing can be pursued without currency risk by using ETFs that employ currency hedging, and so on.

Finally, the rise of liquid alternative ETFs has opened up multi-asset and derivative strategies, with improved liquidity and generally lower fees over mutual funds or separate accounts. ETFs here are benchmarked to indexes that replicate the performance of hedge funds, long–short equity strategies, and liquid private equity. Other categories available include market-neutral, managed futures, multi-alternative, and volatility-based strategies.

ETFs as a Disruptive Innovation

In some ways, the growth of the ETF market is a manifestation of the battle for the heart and soul of investing. ETFs have boosted index-based investing tremendously. Their widespread adoption has the potential to shake up legacy practices that have been entrenched in asset management for many years—including the role of consultants in finding investment products, mutual fund distribution through financial advisers and registered investment advisers, and the central role of actively managed, bottom-up stock and bond management.

In summary, it is not hyperbole to say that ETFs have changed the face of investing. With lower fees, greater transparency, expanded access, and greater tax efficiency than traditional mutual funds, they are attracting assets from those funds and threatening classic fund distribution models. With ETFs' inherent liquidity, they are also altering the trading landscape by providing a market where hedge funds, pension funds, and other institutional investors can connect their order flow with that of high-net-worth and other individual investors and can engage in price discovery for illiquid assets.

ETFs have also made top-down and cross-market investing more accessible by providing tools that can be used in asset or sector allocation, factor-tilt strategies, and thematic investing. They have helped many investors incorporate dynamic strategies into their portfolio management processes by allowing them to adapt to shifting return and risk opportunities. Broadly, ETFs are encouraging a new approach to investing that focuses on macroeconomic and thematic developments rather than single-stock investing. And as a product without a load-based commission structure, ETFs are also accelerating the transition to fee-based fiduciary adviser–investor relationships.

Nevertheless, obstacles still impede ETF asset growth, and if the obstacles are removed, the adoption of ETFs will accelerate. In the United States, major obstacles are the inability of most 401(k)/defined-contribution investment programs to handle ETFs and the lack of expertise in ETF analysis among the institutional consulting community. In addition, the current regulatory framework allows for ETF issuance and trading as a subcategory of *both* mutual fund and equity products, creating a Byzantine approval and oversight environment.

Over the past few years, instances of backlash against ETFs and their role in the marketplace have occurred. People have accused them of corrupting the price discovery mechanism of the stock market, of posing a systemic risk to finance, and of steering investors into inappropriate and complex investments. In the end, the harshest parts of these criticisms do not hold water. But they do highlight that whenever a new and disruptive technology comes along, significant and in-depth education is needed. ETFs are powerful tools that offer lower costs, expand strategic choices, and provide ease of access with transparency. When investors use ETFs appropriately, they can improve their return–risk profiles. Like any powerful tool, however, ETFs can be dangerous if not properly understood.

The complete book can be found at
www.cfapubs.org/toc/rf/2015/2015/3.

Use your mobile device to scan the QR code to go straight to the webpage.

TRADING AND ELECTRONIC MARKETS: WHAT INVESTMENT PROFESSIONALS NEED TO KNOW (A SUMMARY)

by Larry Harris, CFA
Summary prepared by Larry Harris

Many financial problems involve trading in organized markets. Solving these problems successfully requires that traders effectively execute orders while appropriately controlling their transaction costs. This book provides buy-side financial analysts, investment managers, and investment sponsors with the tools to understand and manage recent innovations in trading that involve the automation of both trading systems and trading strategies.

The Implications of the Zero-Sum Game

Investing is a zero-sum game when performance is measured relative to the value-weighted market index. If some investors beat the market, others must underperform. Because investors incur transaction costs when they trade, investing—especially active investing—is a negative-sum game. Controlling transaction costs thus is essential for investors who seek to beat the market or their peers.

The observation that trading is a zero-sum game (or a negative-sum game when transaction costs are included) has an extremely important implication for active investment managers who base their trading decisions on financial analyses. Those managers who regularly underperform the market do not do so because they systematically choose the wrong securities to hold in their portfolios. Being systematically wrong requires as much skill as being systematically right. Rather, managers who regularly underperform lose simply because they trade.

In a zero-sum game, well-informed traders cannot profit from trading with one another. Active investment managers can profit only if other traders are willing to trade with them.

Understanding the reasons why people trade thus can help investment managers and risk managers improve their investment discipline. The most successful managers trade only when they expect that trading will advance their mission, which requires that they understand both why they are trading and why others may lose to them.

The text identifies various reasons for trading. Many people trade because they obtain some benefit besides profits when trading. Investors and borrowers move money forward or backward in time, risk managers transfer risk to others, and gamblers obtain excitement and stories to tell from their trading activities. In contrast, profit-motivated traders trade only because they expect to profit. They profit from analyzing fundamental information better than others do, from obtaining new information before others do, from dealing with other traders, or from anticipating the orders that other traders have submitted or will submit.

Investment managers who trade on information need to know when they can expect to profit. Well-informed traders can profit only when price is different from fundamental value. Since prices generally are close to fundamental values, informed traders can profit only when (1) prices change and fundamental values do not or (2) fundamental values change and prices do not. The first case occurs when uninformed traders cause prices to change. The traders most likely to recognize these opportunities are analysts who estimate fundamental values. The second case occurs when events cause fundamental values to change. Traders who collect news are the first to learn about such events.

The competition among informed traders seeking trading profits causes prices to be informative. As prices become more informative, the opportunities for further speculative trading profits decrease. The number of informed traders and their profits thus depend on the costs of acquiring and processing information and on the total liquidity available to informed traders.

Prices can never fully incorporate all available information. If they did, informed traders would not invest in information that is costly to acquire; if informed traders did not collect that information and trade on it, prices would not be informative. Active investment management thus must be profitable—but only for those traders who can most efficiently collect and process information and only in markets where other traders are willing to trade with them.

Uninformed traders lose on average to well-informed traders simply because they trade. If they trade directly with informed traders, they are on the wrong side of the market. If they trade on the same side, their orders tend not to execute (and they wish that they did) or their trades are very expensive. And if they trade through dealers, they lose because dealers widen their bid and ask prices to recover from all traders what they lose to informed traders.

For uninformed traders, the single most important determinant of their overall transaction costs is the decision to trade. Uninformed traders who do not trade do not lose to informed traders. This observation explains why passive buy-and-hold investment strategies, such as indexing, have grown so popular in recent years.

Transaction Cost Measurement and Management

Effective control of transaction costs requires that they be measured. Buy-side traders and the developers of algorithms measure transaction costs to

1. determine whether their brokers are working effectively on their behalf and to confirm that they are getting value for their brokerage commissions,

2. determine whether they should be trading more or less aggressively,

3. better understand whether they are competing with other traders who are trading on the same information,

4. inform their portfolio managers about liquidity conditions in various securities, and

5. design and fine-tune trading algorithms.

The text explains how analysts measure transaction costs and use them to improve their trading processes.

The best measure of implicit transaction costs (market impact) is the implementation shortfall method, which compares trade prices with prices that stood when the trades were first ordered. The VWAP (volume-weighted average price) method, which managers commonly use, has many problems.

Keeping track of the opportunity costs associated with trades ordered but not executed is very important because this information can help traders know when they should trade more aggressively. Effective two-way communication between portfolio managers and their buy-side traders is also very important to improving investment performance.

Electronic Trading

Trading at organized exchanges now depends critically on the automated electronic systems that exchanges and their trader clients use. Electronic trading systems arrange trades by matching orders submitted by buyers with those submitted by sellers. Many traders—especially dealers and arbitrageurs—use electronic systems to generate the orders that the exchanges process.

Innovative electronic trading systems—and the trading strategies that they facilitate—substantially decrease buy-side transaction costs. But some strategies that high-speed traders use to exploit other traders hurt large traders. Investors can protect themselves from losses to these parasitic traders through some simple trading strategies.

In comparison to floor-based trading systems, electronic order-matching systems enjoy many advantages. Most obviously, electronic systems are very cheap to operate once built. They do exactly what they are programmed to do. They keep perfect audit trails. Electronic exchange systems that support hidden orders keep those orders perfectly hidden—unlike floor brokers, who may inadvertently or fraudulently reveal their clients' hidden orders to friends or confederates. Electronic order-matching systems do not get tired, call in sick, complain about their bonuses, or drop pizza crumbs into their keyboards. And they operate when bad weather or other events can prevent workers from convening on a floor. These efficiencies have allowed electronic trading systems to displace floor-based trading systems in almost all instruments for which order-driven markets are viable.

The proliferation of exchange electronic trading systems has led to the adoption of electronic trading strategies by proprietary traders, buy-side traders, and the electronic brokers that serve them. Proprietary traders include dealers, arbitrageurs, and various types of front runners—all of whom are profit-motivated traders. In contrast, buy-side traders trade to fill orders for investment and risk managers who use the markets to establish positions from which they derive various utilitarian and profit-motivated benefits. Electronic brokers serve both types of traders.

Electronic trading strategies are most profitable or effective when they act on new information quickly. Accordingly, proprietary traders and electronic brokers build automated trading systems that are extremely fast. These systems often can receive and process information and place a trading instruction at an exchange in less than a few milliseconds and sometimes much faster.

High-frequency traders (HFTs) generally complete round trips composed of a purchase followed by a sale (or vice versa) within a minute and often as quickly as a few milliseconds. During the course of a day, they may trade in and out of an actively traded security or contract more than a thousand times but usually only in small sizes. The most common high-frequency-trading strategies are dealing and arbitrage.

Low-latency traders include traders who trade on electronic news feeds and certain parasitic traders. When trying to open or close positions, they often need to send or cancel orders very quickly in response to new information, but they may hold their positions for as long as a day and sometimes longer.

Electronic news traders subscribe to high-speed electronic news feeds that report news releases from corporations, governments, and other aggregators of information. News traders profit when they can trade with stale orders that do not yet reflect the new information.

Most large buy-side traders use electronic order management systems (OMSs) to manage their trading. These systems keep track of the orders that portfolio managers want filled, which orders have been sent out to be filled, and which fills have already been obtained.

Buy-side traders often employ electronic brokers to arrange their trades. In addition to supporting standard order instructions, such as limit or market orders, these brokers often provide a full suite of advanced orders, trading tactics, and algorithms. The brokers' electronic trading systems generally manage these advanced orders, tactics, and algorithms, but in some cases, exchanges may perform these functions.

A *trading tactic* is a plan for executing a simple function that generally involves the submission of multiple orders. A pegged hidden sell order set to always float one tick below the best offer is an example of a common trading tactic.

Algorithms are programmed strategies for filling orders. Algorithms may use combinations or sequences of simple orders, advanced orders, or trading tactics to achieve their objectives. Many algorithms break up large orders and submit the pieces to various markets over time to make it difficult for other traders to infer that a trader is trying to fill a large order. Good algorithms generally obtain low-cost executions by knowing when and where to offer liquidity via limit orders, when to use market orders, and how to most effectively keep the market from becoming aware of their efforts. They reduce the price impacts of large trades.

Electronic traders use many methods to improve their trading. They may hide their orders, use very small orders to discover hidden orders, and repeatedly cancel and resubmit their orders. They often train their systems using machine-learning methods.

Electronic traders must be fast to trade effectively, regardless of whether they are proprietary traders or buy-side traders. Electronic traders have three needs for speed: They must (1) take a trading opportunity before they lose it to others, (2) submit orders before others to be first in line, and (3) cancel orders they no longer want to fill before someone else fills them.

Electronic traders do not need to be fast to trade effectively—they just need to be *faster* than their competitors. The reason electronic trading systems are now so incredibly fast is that electronic traders have been trying for years to be faster than their competitors. To trade quickly, electronic traders buy high-speed data links, use very fast computers that they locate next to exchange servers, write highly efficient code, and often preplan their responses to new information.

Computers have come to dominate the implementation of many trading strategies because they are so efficient and so unlike human traders. They can continuously watch and respond to information from many instruments and many markets simultaneously. Their responses to new information are extraordinarily fast. They do only what they are instructed to do, and they are not forgetful. The efficiency of electronic trading strategies has led to their widespread adoption by proprietary traders, buy-side traders, and brokers—and to substantial drops in transaction costs for both retail and institutional traders.

Practitioner and Regulatory Issues Associated with Fast Electronic Markets

The text concludes with extensive discussions about nine issues associated with fast electronic markets that concern practitioners and regulators.

1. Does speed help capital formation? No one makes capital allocation decisions in milliseconds, but the liquidity offered in fast secondary markets makes new issues more attractive.

2. The competition among HFTs has created an arms race in which each trader tries to be faster than the next. The high costs of HFT technologies make entry quite costly and suggest that successful incumbents may someday be protected from further competition.

3. Many traders believe that high-speed markets are unfair because electronic traders can see and react to more information—and sooner—than can manual traders. Whether this advantage is fair depends on the values of the observer. Some traders have always had better access to the markets than others.

4. Electronic trading has created systemic risks that concern regulators and practitioners. Developers must be extremely careful when instructing their machines to ensure that the machines do only what the developers want and not what they do not expect. Traders, brokers, and exchanges must all surveil order flows to ensure that they are appropriate.

5. Exchanges earn substantial profits from selling high-speed proprietary data feeds to HFTs, often to the disadvantage of traders with slower access. These sales allow exchanges to extract some of the profits that HFTs make from orders that other traders send to exchanges.

6. In many countries, people can trade stocks away from established exchanges in dark pools and through internalizing dealers. Off-exchange trading concerns many

practitioners and regulators because it fragments trading, making it more difficult to find liquidity. If it grows too large, it could imperil price formation.

7. *Maker-taker pricing* is a pricing model that some electronic exchanges use to price their order-matching services. Takers of liquidity pay high exchange fees that subsidize rebates to liquidity makers. This model and its related converse, taker-maker pricing, have created substantial agency problems. Together, they have decreased the tick size to one-half cent for sophisticated traders in US equity markets.

8. Some parasitic electronic trading strategies allow clever traders to exploit public investors, especially those trading large orders. Several changes in market structure can protect these investors, who can also take actions to protect themselves.

9. Some exchanges have created special order types that appeal to HFTs and that sometimes disadvantage slower traders. Traders need to be aware of these orders when considering where to route their orders.

Conclusion and Appendix

The text concludes with some suggestions for simple changes in bond market structure that could substantially decrease transaction costs. Investors would be much better off if they could see a national best bid or offer consolidated from various electronic bond-trading systems, as they can for equities. They also would benefit if brokers allowed them to place limit orders on such systems.

The book concludes with an appendix that identifies the causes of the Flash Crash of 2010 and reports what regulators and traders have done to reduce the probability and magnitude of recurrences.

The complete book can be found at www.cfapubs.org/toc/rf/2015/2015/4.

Use your mobile device to scan the QR code to go straight to the webpage.

THE INDUSTRIAL ORGANIZATION OF THE GLOBAL ASSET MANAGEMENT BUSINESS (A SUMMARY)

by Ingo Walter
Summary prepared by Ingo Walter

The global asset management industry is anything but simple. The key fiduciaries acting for the ultimate beneficiaries include pension funds, endowed institutions, sovereign wealth funds, and individuals. Asset managers—the agents—include investment management firms, insurance companies, mutual funds, and alternative asset firms (e.g., hedge funds and private equity firms).

The dynamics of the asset management business are both complex and geographically diverse. Products and vendors compete within and across clients and markets and often shade into each other. Regulation also can differ dramatically across financial systems and functions, even when pursuing the same objectives of efficiency, growth, and stability on the "buy side" of the financial architecture.

The asset management industry is likely to be one of the largest and most dynamic segments of the global financial services industry in the years ahead. As of early 2015, the global total of assets under management was estimated at close to US$74 trillion including pension fund assets and funds managed by the insurance industry, mutual fund assets, and alternative investment vehicles and private wealth management, but excluding sovereign wealth funds and external reserves of central banks. Not only is this already massive industry likely to grow faster than other parts of the financial services sector, but also cross-border volume—both regional and global—is likely to take an increasing share of that activity.

Within this high-growth context, asset management attracts competitors from an extraordinarily broad range of strategic groups: commercial and universal banks, investment banks, trust companies, insurance companies, private banks, captive and independent pension fund managers, mutual fund companies, and various types of specialist firms. This rich array of contenders—marked by very different starting points, skill sets, competitive resources, and strategic objectives—is likely to render the asset management market highly competitive, even though one can foresee a certain amount of consolidation in some sectors around the world.

This book provides an overview of the global institutional asset management industry. It includes a discussion of the competitive structure, conduct, and performance of the asset management industry as well as an assessment of the impact of institutional asset management on global capital markets.

Living Down the Recent Past

With the passing of the global financial crisis, many things have changed in finance, particularly the asset management industry. As we now know, major financial shocks can no longer be contained. They spread with amazing speed, both geographically and across asset classes and financial intermediaries. Financial interconnectedness can bring great benefits, but it also generates large systemic risks, and there are few places to seek refuge from its consequences. Nor is the real economy spared, with the global aftereffects of the deepest and longest recession since the 1930s still (almost a decade after the Lehman Brothers collapse that arguably defined the peak of the crisis) reflected in sluggish economic growth in many developed countries, delayed capital expenditures, persistently high unemployment, and intractable fiscal deficits among countries in Europe and among states and municipalities elsewhere.

As expected, the asset management industry has not been spared. Massive losses starting in 2007 affected the size of assets managed by almost all fund managers except for a few hedge funds that correctly bet against the asset classes that declined. As we now know, banks were heavily exposed to the toxic assets they were intermediating, assuming "warehousing risk" as investors in addition to "pipeline risk exposure" as financial intermediaries.

Why? Because the "carry trade" was at the time highly profitable given the low regulatory risk weightings assigned to the higher tranches of these structured securities. This became the main source of the banking "crisis," which then led to forced mergers, nationalizations, and taxpayer bailouts—ironically sparing the asset management industry even greater losses—the impact of which continues today.

For the asset management business as a whole, the most pressing challenge is the loss of investor confidence resulting from the financial crisis. In addition, there is increased competition from low-cost providers, including "liquid alternative" providers that claim to deliver hedge fund–like returns without the liquidity limitations of traditional hedge funds. In addition, managers face increased government regulation and intervention in the markets. The opportunity for growth lies with those enterprises that are most able to meet these challenges by providing transparency to their clients, their stakeholders, and, in particular, their regulators. Those that can meet these challenges will be the most effective in the future. Specifically, the industry's challenges can be grouped into three categories: growth, risk management, and cost control.

The Pension Sector

Challenges associated with risk, cost, and growth are interrelated and affect pension funds and pension-related insurance funds to varying degrees. Changing demographics will alter pension-funding patterns, creating both cost challenges and growth opportunities for pension funds, insurance reserves, and those who manage these asset pools.

Greater market volatility, increased financial instability, and material regulatory changes will affect business risk, cost, and growth, respectively, creating challenges as well as opportunities that are not necessarily always equally important. The main drivers of success will be flexibility in strategic targeting and implementation, together with the adaptability of operations.

Scale, internationalization, and the right choice of operational platform are key determinants in promoting growth, mitigating risk, and controlling costs. Functional breadth in terms of retirement products is important, but large size (in terms of assets under management) is also advantageous. Not only the investment side but also the transaction side and the information platform need to be well managed in terms of client services, risk management, and cost efficiency.

Indeed, the operational platform is a common thread running through all the themes related to pension fund asset management. This platform is critical in promoting flexibility and in creating barriers to entry and exit that are central in determining the organization of the industry.

Mutual Funds

Mutual funds emerged from the financial turbulence of 2007–2009 with their reputations among clients severely stressed. Almost all had failed to protect their investors from the broad market decline and increased volatility that accompanied the crisis. This outcome was perceived by many investors as a disaster, despite the stated intentions of many of the funds to move with the overall market, including in periods of decline.

Some funds incorporated structured financial products that they themselves failed to understand—and could not explain adequately to clients—while several major funds prevented their customers from redeeming their shares to avoid having to sell the underlying securities in disorderly markets. Others were lacking in the key areas of due diligence and risk management. The asset management industry as a whole was found deficient in transparency, effective risk control, and operating efficiency, compounding the traditional challenge of producing significant and durable excess returns.

Consequently, the postcrisis era began with the industry facing skeptical, sharp-eyed, and cost-conscious investors who had not forgotten their recent experience, together with low-cost asset management alternatives and demanding regulatory changes.

So, the initial challenge has been to rebuild confidence in mutual funds and other collective investment vehicles while dealing with intensified competition from several quarters and formulating a constructive set of responses to the inevitable increase in regulatory pressure—some of which remains highly uncertain. The emphasis is on improved transparency at all levels—products, processes, costs, and compliance—and a fundamental reconsideration by top management of these issues as sources of competitive advantage rather than as purely defensive challenges.

Mutual funds able to meet these challenges—in the face of competition from passive funds, hedge funds, and a number of nontraditional competitors—are likely to be most prominent among the winners in a world where business as usual is unlikely to produce the kind of growth, risk profile, or operating efficiency the industry has enjoyed in the past.

The mutual fund management industry also needs to prepare for still further pressure on fees. Active managers in particular are under fee pressure from index funds and exchange-traded funds (ETFs), from government regulation, and from alternative investments. Passive index funds and ETFs guarantee "beta" returns for very low fees, whereas alternatives provide the opportunity to access "alpha" returns at high fees. So, active mutual funds that charge high fees and produce little (or negative) alpha but plenty of beta are caught in the middle. And there seems to be a certain amount of convergence, with some active funds cutting fees and producing market returns and some passive funds and ETFs promising "index plus" returns, using sector selection approaches, and charging higher fees for the added value.

Alternative Assets

This book focuses on two components of the alternative assets sector: hedge funds and private equity funds. Some other asset classes are usually considered alternatives, including real estate and commodities. Here we emphasize the hedge fund industry because of its global growth and its size in terms of assets under management, as well as the performance and regulatory issues that confront the industry. Besides wealthy individuals, institutions have become large investors in both types of alternatives, although high fees and disclosure problems have moderated their participation of late.

Hedge funds may or may not hedge. The classic model of a hedge fund is one that invests in long positions in assets that the manager thinks will rise in price and short positions in those thought likely to fall—a "long–short" strategy (which may or may not be market-neutral, that is, balanced so that the overall fund is insensitive to market movements). This model persists, but it is only one of many hedge fund strategies, and unlike the long–short strategy, they may or may not involve hedging.

In the wake of the global financial crisis, the hedge fund industry has made a concerted effort to restore investor confidence while dealing with intensified competition from several quarters and formulating a constructive set of responses to the increased regulatory pressure that inevitably follows financial trauma. Much of the emphasis will have to be on improved transparency at all levels—products, processes, costs, and compliance—and a fundamental reconsideration by top management of these issues as sources of competitive advantage rather than purely defensive measures.

A particular area of concern is operational risk. Operational risk issues reached their peak in the Bernie Madoff and Bear Stearns episodes, including the need for serious external audits by firms exposed to high levels of reputational risk, stress testing for both liquidity and earnings streams, the structure of incentives, and the problem of risk aggregation in its transmission to senior management and boards.

Legal and regulatory risks are part of this mosaic, as is the application of a good dose of common sense alongside traditional and proprietary risk modeling. Equally important are rigorous cost-accounting discipline—an area in which firms have often been found wanting in their rush to boost assets under management—and operating leverage in the face of high fixed costs and variable revenues as well as trading costs and uncertainty about the importance of economies of scale.

Given the difficulty of persistent outperformance in any management structure, including hedge funds, costs are a critical competitive element and require imaginative outsourcing, application of world-class technology, and, in some cases, serious conversations with clients about appropriate fee structures. Asset management has bright growth prospects worldwide. But unless risk and efficiency are addressed more effectively than in the past at a given firm, its competitors could be the main beneficiary of that growth.

Hedge funds and other alternative asset managers able to meet these challenges in the face of stiff, nontraditional competition are likely to be most prominent among the winners in a world where business as usual is unlikely to produce the kind of growth, risk profile, or operating efficiency that hedge funds have enjoyed in the past.

Before the financial crisis, the alternative asset management enterprise was very different from what it is today. Businesses were able to survive with very high cost structures. Now, we are seeing a need to control costs and a need to be transparent within the organization regarding the nature of the products being sold and the magnitude of the costs necessary to offer those products.

Private Clients

Global individual wealth can take a variety of forms, encompassing financial assets (currency, bank balances, stocks, bonds, etc.) and real assets—commodities, precious stones, *objets d'art*, real estate, and other asset classes that have some sort of actual or potential market value. These assets range across the entire liquidity, risk, and return spectrum, from cash to real estate to private equity investments. The ability to measure wealth at any point in time depends on the existence of a market for each asset (hence, the importance of liquidity) and the ability to "mark to market." Because wealthy individuals' assets are often held in illiquid form, global wealth estimates tend to be somewhat inaccurate. A variety of intermediaries are engaged in wealth management, including trust companies, major banks and financial conglomerates, investment banks, private banks and boutiques, individual financial advisers, and single- and multi-family offices. Market shares are highly fragmented, and wealthy investors have plenty of choice.

The essential factor is to offer a truly personal service that focuses on the asset side and sometimes on the liability side of the client's balance sheet. Moreover, owing to the highly personal nature of private banking, clients generally prefer to "stay with" a particular firm, if possible, resulting in a lower price and performance sensitivity, facilitating product cross-selling, and enabling institutions to compete on qualitative variables instead of pricing alone. The business is "capital light," with favorable cost-to-income ratios and the capability to realize significant economies of scale in transaction-processing and portfolio management activities.

The bundling of private wealth management services makes it difficult to evaluate the value/cost relationship of each component, potentially allowing the firm to extract higher fees. And the client is likely to be less price sensitive with respect to the purchase of bundled services than with respect to the purchase of each service separately.

Although other areas of banking have been subject to a general unbundling of services as a result of a proliferation of new financial products and techniques, private banking remains an area where bundling may retain value for some time to come. And owing to the existence of economies of scope, a bank can often provide several services more economically than it can provide a single service—an important rationale for the cross-selling of bank products. Since the fiduciary nature of the private wealth management relationship gives the bank access to a rich vein of client-specific information, it may retain an advantage in servicing the private client that competitors find difficult to penetrate.

The apex of private wealth management is arguably the "family office," which manages investment and trust assets for a single family, staffed by professionals in various aspects of wealth management committed to the family's (often complex and changing) financial objectives. A variant is the multiple-family office, which serves several wealthy families in managing segregated, but sometimes pooled, investment accounts. Key issues include intergenerational wealth transfers, fiduciary obligations in trust relationships, fees paid to external asset managers, and tax efficiency. Traditional family offices may also provide such personal services as managing household staff and making travel arrangements. Other services typically handled by the traditional family office include property management, accounting and payroll functions, and management of legal affairs. Family offices often handle philanthropy activities as well.

Performance Issues

What is required to excel in the asset management industry? Significant distribution in leading markets, product breadth and consistency, global money management expertise, and capital strength lie at the core. Also needed are technology capability, marketing and customer service skills, defensible pricing, low-cost production, and a strong brand. All this must be rooted in an affirmative culture, cohesive senior management, and a talented and motivated staff.

Despite the complexity reflected throughout this book, the common threads that run through the discussion—growth, risk, and cost—cannot be ignored by asset managers hoping to be sustainable in the market. Sustainable competitive performance for firms in the asset management business may involve accessing sometimes unfamiliar markets to generate growth, managing all kinds of risk (market, credit, and liquidity risk as well as sovereign, operational, and reputational risk), and paying careful attention to cost control in an environment where persistent outperformance is exceedingly difficult. Still, the future looks bright. Each year, massive investable funds arise that have to be deployed in the best interests of their owners—the core mandate of this industry.

The complete book can be found at
www.cfapubs.org/toc/rf/2015/2015/5.

Use your mobile device to scan the QR code to go straight to the webpage.

III. LITERATURE REVIEW SUMMARIES

LONGEVITY RISK AND RETIREMENT INCOME PLANNING (A SUMMARY)

by Patrick J. Collins, CFA, Huy D. Lam, CFA, and Josh Stampfli
Summary prepared by Patrick J. Collins, CFA, Huy D. Lam, CFA, and Josh Stampfli

Investors face the challenge of designing and implementing financial asset portfolios capable of providing adequate income throughout their lifetime. This task requires prudent decision making regarding selection of a suitable retirement age, portfolio asset allocations, standard of living targets, precautionary savings amounts, and portfolio withdrawal strategies. Longevity risk—the economic consequences of outliving financial resources—is a critical factor in quantifying the risk–return trade-offs embedded in these asset management decisions. When a finite amount of capital must provide lifetime income, portfolio management often becomes a tug of war between capital preservation (terminal wealth) and lifetime spending (consumption).

A substantial and ever-growing body of research from actuaries, financial economists, trustees and their legal advisers, and investment advisers reflects the challenge of designing, implementing, and monitoring portfolios capable of providing adequate lifetime income. The accretion of publications over the 50-year period from 1965 through 2014 engenders a need to provide a chronological and thematic survey of this research. Incorporated into the CFA Institute Research Foundation literature review are an extensive bibliography of relevant studies, references to supplemental surveys on specialized topics, and reference to an annotated bibliography providing more technical, in-depth discussions of both academic and practitioner-produced literature. We have selected a chronological format because it is instructive to see, over time, how issues and research methods wax and wane. A strictly thematic structure would have pushed the narrative closer to an intellectual history. Such a book, however, would mask the flavor of research endeavors. Disparate topics in seemingly unrelated areas emerge, over time, in actuarial or academic journals written for differing readerships. From time to time, research efforts achieve a synthesis that provides promising insights into issues of common interest. The chronological aspect of the literature survey conveys a better sense of a study's importance and originality because it places it in the context of previous investigations and commentary.

The survey is divided into four sections.

Introduction

The beginning section orients the reader to the intellectual landscape that we survey. We define longevity risk and briefly discuss the economic implication of longer lifespans. A critical issue is whether financial asset portfolios can provide adequate cash throughout the investor's lifespan. One alternative to funding retirement through a financial asset portfolio is to implement an actuarial solution—that is, to annuitize some or all of investment wealth. Annuities appear in the literature in a variety of ways: (1) optimal consumption paths, (2) guides to self-annuitization investment strategies, (3) benchmarks for assessing portfolio performance, (4) cost-of-retirement proxies, (4) portfolio solvency benchmarks, and (5) contracts that compete for the investor's dollar within a marketplace of financial instruments.

Having provided an overview of the various contexts in which annuities appear, we briefly discuss how researchers project the likelihood that a portfolio, operating under a jointly specified asset allocation and periodic withdrawal strategy, will produce a financially successful retirement over a possibly stochastic time horizon. Our introduction focuses primarily on historical back testing and introduces the concept of model risk—that is, the risk that a model may produce spurious probability assessments. We then acquaint the reader with the complexities of introducing dynamic asset allocation and spending strategies into a retirement income risk model. Complexity increases by an order of magnitude as a model incorporates various asset management elections (buy and hold, constant mix, insured portfolio, and so forth) and dynamic spending rules.

With this background in hand, we then discuss risk measures that can serve as portfolio preferencing metrics, including (1) assessments of past investment results with performance evaluation metrics, such as the Sharpe ratio, the information ratio, and Jensen's alpha; (2) shortfall risk metrics (the preference is the asset allocation/spending strategy that exhibits the lowest likelihood of portfolio depletion during the planning horizon), which are based on the outputs of models designed to project future portfolio values; and (3) solvency metrics, which are based on current observables (the current market value of assets relative to the current cost of an annuity providing target income for life).

There are two basic types of retirement income models. Life-cycle models encompass a range of approaches in which investors use information to make sequential decisions to attain financial objectives. Most life-cycle models use a utility (welfare) criterion as an asset management preferencing metric. The life-cycle approach assigns weights to both consumption and terminal wealth utility, and the model identifies the asset management strategy producing the greatest aggregate utility value over the planning horizon. Shortfall minimization models test the ability of various asset management elections to achieve targeted income and terminal wealth. Historical backtests, bootstrapped reshuffling of historical returns, and Monte Carlo simulations of pre-parameterized distributions are popular methods of assessing shortfall likelihood and magnitude.

Finally, some retirement income models incorporate a solvency or feasibility metric. The feasibility condition requires that the current market value of assets equals the stochastic present value of the lifetime target income plus, if relevant, gifts and bequests. A critical distinction is drawn between *sustainability*—the probability, calculated by a risk model, that future financial market returns are sufficient to defease targeted cash flows—and *feasibility*, a judgment regarding the current ability of the portfolio to fund the present value of required cash flows. Monitoring the feasibility condition differs from assessing a portfolio's financial health in terms of the likelihood of sustainability over the planning horizon. Unlike the shortfall probability metric, which is the risk model's best guess, the feasibility condition is a function of current market observables.

The advances in modeling described throughout this literature survey facilitate prudent portfolio surveillance and monitoring in terms of utility, shortfall, and feasibility risk metrics. Over time, the locus of action in retirement income planning shifts from a search for the best portfolio design and spending rules to dynamic portfolio monitoring and intelligent assessment of asset management decisions.

Retirement Income Risk Models (1965–2005)

The origin of many academic commentaries can be traced to Yaari (1965).[1] Yaari demonstrates that investors without a bequest objective and with access to actuarially fair annuities in a complete market setting—one where insurance or financial instruments span all economic risks faced by the investor—will hold all wealth in "actuarial notes." Yaari considers how the investor can optimize discounted expected utility over both a deterministic period and an uncertain lifespan where the investor places a value on both consumption and bequests. Investors lacking a bequest objective will maximize a utility function for consumption only, and their challenge is to find the optimal feasible consumption plan when the planning horizon is uncertain. Under the Yaari complete market model, annuities put the investor on the optimal feasible consumption path.

[1]Menahem E. Yaari, "Uncertain Lifetime, Life Insurance, and the Theory of the Consumer," *Review of Economic Studies*, vol. 32, no. 2 (April 1965): 137–150.

Although Yaari's (1965) classic paper is also an important source document for researchers applying a portfolio shortfall probability risk metric, Yaari does not develop a probability-of-success approach to evaluating portfolio choice. Rather, he evaluates investment and actuarial solutions in terms of maximizing investor utility (welfare) over the applicable planning horizon at an appropriate discount rate for a risk-averse investor manifesting a possibly time-varying preference for consumption as a function of age. Yaari's model sets the table for future inquiry in that it acknowledges (1) the usefulness of both utility-based life-cycle modeling and shortfall risk modeling; (2) the existence of both actuarial- and investment-oriented solutions; and (3) the importance of the consumer's preference function ("impatience") with respect to the timing and magnitude of retirement spending. It is not an exaggeration to state that future research papers seek to test, extend, and sharpen Yaari's insights.

We note the appearance of asset/liability matching models that, in turn, introduce new metrics for evaluating a portfolio's financial health and its likelihood for long-term success. One example is the wealth/consumption ratio, which improves or deteriorates over time according to various asset allocation/spending elections. This period also sees the introduction of an option valuation approach to portfolio management. For example, models seek to provide insight, under various economic circumstances and investor conditions, into the optimal time to exercise the option to annuitize wealth.

Modeling becomes more dynamic, investment and actuarial solutions are closely compared and evaluated in terms of utility and shortfall risk preferencing metrics, and a greater premium is placed on ongoing and active portfolio monitoring. We chronicle a split among commentators on the subject of optimal annuity timing. Some suggest that investors should annuitize all wealth when the annuity contract's mortality premium exceeds the expected premium from holding a risky asset portfolio—an option valuation approach that stresses the fact that annuities are a cost-efficient way to generate income. Others suggest that investors should annuitize all wealth as soon as they can lock in their desired future income stream. Finally, others suggest that, if prudent, investors should delay exercising the option to annuitize. The recommendation to delay stems from the observations that (1) immediate annuitization may impose an unacceptable constraint on future consumption and (2) investors value smoothed marginal utility of lifetime consumption more than a fixed periodic dollar-value income.

In this section, we also document a growing dissatisfaction with how models generate the future paths of investment and inflation processes. Model outputs appear to be unrealistic. Specifically, questions emerge concerning the consequences of

- using models incorporating only the first two moments of the distribution of financial asset returns,
- limiting model input to only one or two risky asset classes,

- assuming complete markets operating under frictionless conditions,
- inputting a constant inflation process,
- limiting the form of the utility function to constant relative risk aversion, and
- failing to incorporate a floor (threshold) lower bound for consumption.

Although this period is one of significant research advances, it is also a period of growing controversy regarding financial planning recommendations as well as increased skepticism regarding the model outputs used to support such recommendations.

Academic Research (2005–2014)

We characterize the research of this period as an effort to relax the rigid and oversimplified assumptions of previous retirement income risk models. Additionally, during this period, risk models incorporate many more variables of interest, including economic shocks (e.g., unreimbursed medical/dental costs), the role of human capital, flexibility in spending and in the selection of a retirement date, the effect of illiquidity on the selection of portfolio assets, and other economic factors. Both the implied and explicit financial planning recommendations appearing in the literature are model dependent, and with the rapid expansion of modeling capabilities, there is a marked increase in the heterogeneity of such recommendations.

One consequence of these developments is of special significance. A large number of articles written for a practitioner audience focused on the issue of how much can be safely withdrawn each year from a retirement income portfolio. These practitioner-oriented articles often resort to pure empiricism in an attempt to parse historical return evolutions to find rules for safe and sustainable portfolio withdrawals. The period 2005–2014, however, saw a marked decrease in the use of risk models based primarily on historical back testing. On one hand, this result is owing to an increasing appreciation of the limitations of this modeling method; on the other, it has much to do with the unexpected virulence of the 2008–09 global recession.

Life-cycle models undergo a similar transformation. They provide valuable insights into complex interactions among longevity, asset allocation, labor income, work/leisure trade-offs, timing of annuitization options, and portfolio withdrawal strategies (investor spending). Furthermore, optimal asset allocation and portfolio management decisions vary substantially across the population of investors depending on (1) the form of the investor's utility of wealth function (e.g., relative or absolute risk aversion) and (2) the degree of investor risk aversion (i.e., the concavity of the utility function). In general, the life-cycle model research of this period shreds conventional wisdom. It rejects the one-size-fits-all rules of portfolio design and safe withdrawal rate management derived from historical back testing. Retirement planning advice changes as models incorporate differing utility of wealth functions, dynamically changing risk aversion, and period-by-period threshold income requirements.

The actuarial literature outlined in the previous section commands increased attention as investigation into the techniques for and costs of producing adequate income throughout the planning horizon becomes an increasingly important topic in a low interest rate environment. At least two issues emerge: (1) a benchmarking issue—to what extent the annuity benchmark represents a reasonable way to compare and contrast retirement income strategies—and (2) a debate regarding the prudence of when and how to annuitize retirement assets. Neither issue is new. However, the incorporation of a threshold income requirement into risk modeling changes the nature of the investigation. Commentators are split on whether to annuitize as soon as possible lest a forthcoming bear market jeopardize the ability to secure threshold income or to delay annuitization to capture the expected risk premium and, potentially, enter into a lower-cost annuity contract issued at an older age. The literature survey describes studies advocating an "annuitize ASAP strategy," as well as studies espousing an "annuity-as-safety-net strategy."

New definitions of prudent asset management emerge alongside new characterizations of risk and portfolio preferencing metrics. The topics of state preference utility, threshold income, consumption variance, maximization of lifetime income, conditional versus unconditional shortfall risk, and subjective discounting to reflect consumer impatience begin to take the forefront in model building. Indeed, the advances in model building during this period are striking. Particularly noteworthy is the emergence of monitoring and performance benchmarks based on a single premium immediate annuity. Such a benchmark shapes new methods for assessing a portfolio's ability to provide needed future funds.

A Survey of Academic Literature on Annuities

We examine several studies that consider the merits of annuitizing some or all of financial wealth to guarantee lifetime periodic income payments. This asset management election is often evaluated in the context of a life-cycle model seeking to gauge the utility value of an actuarially fair annuity. Actuarially fair annuities are, however, unavailable to investors. The prudence of exercising an option to annuitize depends, of course, on a variety of factors, including contract costs. The cost of an actuarial solution determines the capital sacrifice required to transfer longevity risk from the investor to the insurance industry. That is, it quantifies the amount of wealth that must leave the financial asset portion of the retirement portfolio to secure a target amount of periodic lifetime income.

We review a large body of research on the topic of annuity costs and benefits. The initial discussion focuses on academic papers seeking to develop and apply a variety of methods (value per premium dollar, expected present discounted value, internal rate of return, the money's worth ratio, implied annuity yield, and so forth) to estimate the costs and loads of commercially available single premium immediate annuity contracts. The review compares and contrasts cost estimation methods and details the conclusions of a variety of research studies looking at both the US and European annuity markets. Conclusions can vary greatly depending on a number of assumptions regarding interest rate discounting factors, population mortality, and the choice of the utility function for determining the value of annuitization for retired investors.

We further look at how actuaries decompose annuity costs to account for sales compensation, insurance carrier profit objectives, reserve requirements and crediting spreads, adverse selection risk, contract administration, investment opportunities and asset mixes, and other relevant factors. This discussion is more of a bottom-up attempt to quantify annuity costs as opposed to the top-down methodologies found in the academic approaches described in the previous paragraph.

Two additional topics are covered in this section. First, there is a brief discussion of whether annuities are, in fact, risk-free financial instruments. The review includes examples of insurance carrier insolvency, the role of state-sponsored guarantee funds, and the need to diversify the annuity portfolio. Second, we provide a spectrum of opinion regarding the wisdom of purchasing an annuity contract in a low interest rate environment. A concluding section provides final thoughts, and an extensive bibliography follows.

The complete literature review can be found at
www.cfapubs.org/toc/rflr/2015/10/2.

Use your smartphone to scan the QR code to go straight to the webpage.

IV. RF BRIEFS SUMMARIES

INVESTOR RISK PROFILING: AN OVERVIEW (A SUMMARY)

by Joachim Klement, CFA
Summary prepared by Joachim Klement, CFA

Research Foundation Briefs

INVESTOR RISK PROFILING: AN OVERVIEW

- Suitability rules demand that practitioners assess the risk profiles of investors before recommending specific investment products or strategies.
- Current practice of using questionnaires to identify investor risk profiles is inadequate and unreliable, typically explaining less than 15% of the variation in risky assets between investors.
- Research has identified more reliable ways to assess investor risk profiles, such as addressing the environment of an investor as well as her lifetime experiences.
- Identifiable factors can be combined to build reliable risk profiles—something that is increasingly demanded by regulators.

Joachim Klement, CFA

CFA Institute Research Foundation

CELEBRATING 50 YEARS OF RESEARCH

In this discussion of investor risk profiling, current risk-profiling practice is reviewed and contrasted with regulatory demands and recent research findings. The current standard process of risk profiling through questionnaires is found to be highly unreliable and typically explains less than 15% of the variation in risky assets between investors. The cause is primarily the design of the questionnaires, which focus on socio-economic variables and hypothetical scenarios to elicit the investor's behavior.

Existing research in risk profiling shows, however, that several different factors can provide more accurate and reliable insight into the risk profiles of investors. Among these factors are the lifetime experiences of the investor and the financial decisions the investor has made in the past. Another important factor is the influence of family, friends, and advisers. These factors can be identified and used by practitioners to enhance their understanding of client preferences and inform their recommendations of investment strategies and products.

The complete brief can be found at
www.cfapubs.org/toc/rflr/2015/10/1.

Use your mobile device to scan the QR code to go straight to the webpage.

V. MULTIMEDIA SUMMARIES

INVESTMENT MANAGEMENT: A SCIENCE TO TEACH OR AN ART TO LEARN? (AUDIOBOOK SUMMARY)

by Frank J. Fabozzi, CFA, Sergio M. Focardi, and Caroline Jonas
Summary prepared by Frank J. Fabozzi, CFA, Sergio M. Focardi, and Caroline Jonas

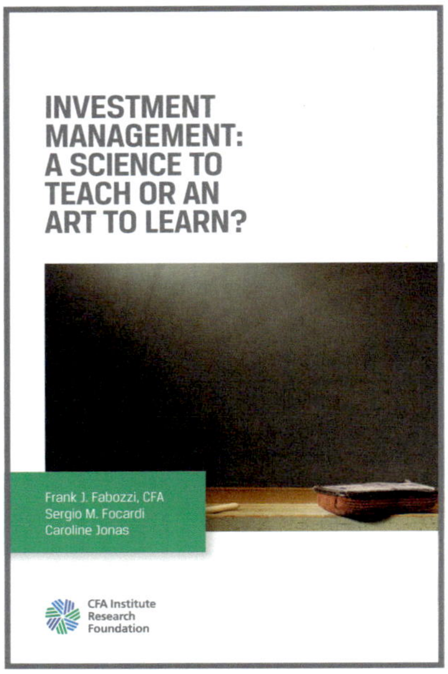

In the aftermath of the 2007–09 financial crisis, mainstream finance theory was criticized for having failed to either prevent or forecast the market crash, which resulted in large losses for investors. Worse, the suggestion was made that the crash itself was the result of bad or poorly applied theory. Although markets have since recovered, surpassing precrisis levels as of the end of 2013, the investors enjoying the recovery are not always the same investors as those who suffered the losses. So, in many cases, the crash caused permanent impairment of wealth.

This crash is particularly interesting in that finance theory, not simply the practices of the financial services industry, has been directly blamed. This book explores current critiques of mainstream theory and discusses implications for the curricula of finance programs at business schools and universities. It is based on conversations with academics and practitioners in the industry and a review of the literature.[1]

Has mainstream finance theory—which many consider an idealization that does not take into account market reality—failed investors? Do we need to reconsider the theory and how it is taught?

[1]The full book contains a list of persons whose opinions (expressed either in interviews or in publicly available documents) are cited in the book. The many gracious human resources managers at asset management firms who helped us were promised anonymity and are not listed.

Editor's note: The print book was published in 2014, and the audiobook was published in 2015.

Finance Theory: Do We Have a Science to Teach?

Many would argue that financial economics belongs not to the realm of empirical natural science but to the realm of the social sciences. Economics and finance have as their subject a human artifact—the economy or the markets—not the laws of nature. The artifact is context specific: It is not independent of social or political objectives. Hence, separating empirical laws from statements of principles is difficult.

Why is mainstream finance theory considered to be so unrealistic by so many? The answer is, not only because its main assumptions—efficient markets, rational expectations, the representative agent, and optimization, which form the basis of general equilibrium theory—are unrealistic but also because the entire theoretical construct is not related to observable quantities. For example, a fundamental theoretical variable, price, is defined as the discounted present value of an infinite stream of future quantities that are not observable. The fact that finance theory makes impossible demands on the knowledge of economic agents is a crucial point that affects all mainstream general equilibrium theories.

In addition to this fundamental issue, the critique of mainstream finance theory can be summarized in three key points:

- First, no real agent has perfect knowledge of the future, not even in a probabilistic sense. Hence, the notion of rational expectations is unrealistic.
- Second, the representative agent is not a sound concept because one cannot aggregate utility functions and obtain a utility function with all the characteristics needed to justify equilibrium.
- Third, economies are rarely in a state of equilibrium. Joseph Stiglitz, professor of economics and University Professor at Columbia University and a corecipient of the 2001 Nobel Prize in Economics, has counted approximately 100 financial crises worldwide in the past 30 years.

Attempts have been made to address these problems within (or alongside) the existing theory. For example, although mainstream economists fail to recognize the existence of bubbles, some observers do attempt to explain market crashes, integrating into finance factors from outside classical finance theory. Specifically, the role of liquidity in the formation of sharp upward and downward market swings is now widely recognized, but will adding liquidity to mainstream finance theory be enough to achieve a complete understanding of markets? A longer list of what is needed to rethink finance theory, taking into consideration the real world, might also include leverage, bad behavior, bad incentives, and delegated management.

As for the role of human behavior in explaining large market swings, Robert Shiller, professor of economics at Yale University and corecipient of the 2013 Nobel Prize in Economics, explored how psychological factors drive stock markets in *Irrational Exuberance*.[2] More recently, he has suggested that bubbles might best be referred to as speculative epidemics: Enthusiasm spreads from person to person like a contagion and, in the process, amplifies stories that might justify asset price increases.[3]

Andrew Lo, professor of finance at MIT's Sloan School of Management, developed what he calls the "adaptive market hypothesis."[4] He argues that by applying the principles of evolution (competition, adaptation, and natural selection) to financial interactions, it is possible to reconcile economic theories based on the efficient market hypothesis with behavioral economics.

Another way to improve finance theory would be to establish a link between financial markets and the real economy—a link that many find lacking in today's theory.

One might ask: Can the debate on the tenability of today's finance theory be resolved with the methods of empirical science? Will the debate remain at the level of dogma, as with the conflict between different views of political economics? Or will the debate remain at the epistemological level, centered on the question of what the cognitive value may be of a model that, in the best case, captures only some general features of the real economy and real markets?

Mainstream economic and finance theories make *probabilistic* predictions, but to test these predictions is difficult when samples are small and contain much noise. The late Fischer Black famously wrote, "Noise makes it very difficult to test either practical or academic theories about the way that financial or economic markets work. We are forced to act largely in the dark."[5]

Ultimately, the debate on general equilibrium models in economics and finance theory may be an empty one. Clearly, general equilibrium models are not empirically validated in terms of the characteristics and interactions of real agents. Given any asset-pricing model that does not admit arbitrage, however, we can always formulate an equivalent abstract general equilibrium model.

If prevailing theory indeed fails to represent the world as it is and has effectively proved to be of little *practical* use, can we consider our economic and finance theory to be hard science? Would it not be better to reinstate economics and finance as *social sciences* (albeit, given the inherently quantitative nature of the data, quantitative social

---

[2]Robert J. Shiller, *Irrational Exuberance* (Princeton, NJ: Princeton University Press, 2000; 2nd ed., 2005).

[3]Robert J. Shiller, "Bubbles Forever," *Project Syndicate* (17 July 2013): http://www.project-syndicate.org/print/the-never-ending-struggle-with-speculative-bubbles-by-robert-j--shiller.

[4]Andrew W. Lo, "The Adaptive Markets Hypothesis," *Journal of Portfolio Management*, vol. 30, no. 5 (30th Anniversary, 2004):15–29.

[5]Fischer Black, "Noise," *Journal of Finance*, vol. 41, no. 3 (July 1986), p. 529.

sciences)? In this case, would we allot a reduced role to complex mathematics and modeling because of the problems with the theory behind the mathematics?

There are two arguments against considering economic and finance theory to be a mathematical science. The first is that economics and finance are dominated by single events that cannot be predicted or even described in mathematical terms. The second argument is that the dynamics of economic and financial phenomena are simply too complex to be captured by mathematical formulas—at least by today's mathematics. Perhaps the phenomena are too complex to admit a parsimonious mathematical description. Forcing "mathematization" can actually impoverish, rather than enrich, knowledge.

The problem is not that economics is too mathematical; the problem is that the mathematics we use in economics is much too simple to capture the complexities of economic interrelationships. This situation calls for greater use of non-mathematical reasoning in managing assets. The likelihood is that economics and financial economics are only partially mathematical theories; they need to be complemented with less formal reasoning. For example, we might not have a lot of data on rare events, such as market crashes and depressions, but we can formulate reasonable scenarios that can, in turn, be mathematically represented.

Whereas some argue that economics and finance should be considered social sciences, others argue for a stricter adherence to the paradigm of empirical science. Again, the impact on the curriculum would not be negligible. The invention of high-performance computers marked a new epoch in the application of mathematics to science and ushered in the application of computational mathematics. Instead of being limited to closed-form solutions of differential equations, we could actually create, through simulation, structures of numbers or symbols that mimic the structure of reality. This advance greatly enlarged the areas of the practical applicability of mathematics. Nevertheless, many complex phenomena, such as the economy, still cannot be represented in detail by using mathematics. Various reasons account for this situation: chaos and sensitivity to initial conditions, objective complexity (the extent to which a phenomenon is close to randomness), and our ignorance of the laws. But these are moving targets.

If we follow the road of stricter adherence to the paradigm of empirical science, we can broadly distinguish three main subfields of scientific economics: (1) econometrics and signal processing applied to financial economics, (2) statistical mechanics applied to economics, and (3) complex system theory and network theory.

Econometrics is the oldest application of scientific principles to economics and finance. It is based on applying statistical methods—in particular, time-series analysis—to empirical data. The key problem is the amount of noise present in empirical finance data, which makes estimates highly uncertain. The diffusion of electronic transactions and the consequent availability of high-frequency and tick-by-tick data have enabled new methods of time-series analysis borrowed from the field of signal processing.

Econometrics and signal processing can be considered applications of the scientific method in restricted domains, such as trading and execution in investment management. These techniques are based on collecting data, constructing hypothetical models, and then testing the models.

The application of statistical mechanics to financial economics is a relatively new field. Of the results obtained, perhaps the best known is the celebrated presence of fat tails in most economic data distributions. Fat tails of distributions imply that large events have a non-negligible probability of happening. Fat tails play a fundamental role in investment management, with important implications for the notions of diversification, risk–return optimization, and risk management.

Network theory is being used to model aggregation and contagion phenomena that may explain crashes. Some researchers argue that with the growing connectivity of economies and markets, aspiring risk managers would do well to study network theory to capture the system dynamics at work in a connected world.

The Theory and Practice of Investment after the Crisis: Need for Change?

Current mainstream finance theory is embodied in general equilibrium models that are idealized mathematical representations of markets populated by rational agents who have perfect knowledge of all possible contingencies now and into the infinite future and who optimize the utility derived from consumption and production. Agents are coordinated solely by price signals.

Even many of the theory's advocates acknowledge that these models are unrealistic (or simplistic) and require the consideration of additional "pieces." Among the additional pieces are the banking system, liquidity, employment and wages, instabilities arising from cascades of interactions, and crises.

The 2007–09 crisis has taught us some lessons. The lessons with relevance to investment management apply mostly to the following categories: diversification, optimization, the capital asset pricing model, the efficient market hypothesis, and risk measurement and risk management.

Diversification

Since the pioneering work of Harry Markowitz, diversification has been a fundamental concept in asset management and asset-pricing theories.[6] From a statistical point of view, diversification is summarized in two mathematical facts: (1) The appropriate

[6]Harry Markowitz, "Portfolio Selection," *Journal of Finance*, vol. 7, no. 1 (March 1952):77–91.

choice of weights—that is, the proportion of funds invested in each asset—can reduce the variance of a portfolio while maintaining unchanged the portfolio's expected return, and (2) the variance of the portfolio that has the minimum possible variance is smaller than the variance of any of its components.

These properties are purely statistical facts and are, of course, undisputed. It is the *effectiveness* of diversification—at every level of aggregation—that has been questioned. Defenders of diversification argue that, although it might occasionally fail because of random fluctuations in market parameters, diversification remains a major component of investment decision making. Critics argue that diversification is ineffective in many economic states, such as when large market swings or crashes occur, because most expected returns in those states are negative. Market parameters change. The key question is how to optimize diversification strategies in markets characterized by changing parameters.

In addition, critics argue that diversification is a mathematical concept that is theoretically valid but whose application is difficult. Diversification requires the estimation—more precisely, a forecast—of the covariance matrix of returns. But the estimation of covariance matrices is subject to many uncertainties. In large portfolios in particular, empirical covariance matrices are very noisy because of the large number of entries.

Optimization

In the methodology of neoclassical finance, "efficient diversification of portfolios" is accomplished through mean–variance optimization (MVO). Broadly, optimization refers to a family of approaches to portfolio construction that include the use of alternative risk measures, such as tracking error and value at risk (VaR), the consideration of transaction costs, portfolio management constraints, and analyzing sensitivity to the estimates of expected returns and covariances.

As with diversification, the mathematics of MVO is not at issue. The question is, Does the mathematics of MVO correspond to the empirical reality of investments? The problem is whether or not we can find, empirically, a meaningful separation between diversifiable, unrewarded risk and non-diversifiable, rewarded risk. The defenders of MVO maintain that we can. Others observe, however, that MVO is of little use because it addresses only "benign" risks—namely, expected fluctuations in asset values as measured by standard deviation. It does not address systemic risks that can result in large losses.

The Capital Asset Pricing Model

The capital asset pricing model (CAPM) is an asset-pricing theory based on the assumption that all investors share the same rational expectations and use mean–variance optimization to choose portfolio weights. The key quantitative finding of the CAPM is that the expected excess return of each asset is proportional to the expected excess return of the market. The proportionality factor is the covariance between the returns of each asset and market returns.

In practice, however, the CAPM is often confused with a one-factor model. Many defenders of the CAPM view the poor performance of the model during the 2007–09 financial crisis as an expression of normal statistical fluctuations. Practitioners who consider the CAPM to be, in practice, a one-factor model observe that a one-factor model is a poor approximation of reality.

The Efficient Market Hypothesis

The efficient market hypothesis (EMH) is made up of two distinct hypotheses: (1) Asset prices have theoretical values (that is, an asset has a "fair price"), and (2) market prices coincide with theoretical prices. The link between the EMH and asset pricing is provided by the notion that the theoretical value of an asset is the present value of its future discounted cash flows. Markets are efficient if the price of each asset equals or comes close to the present value of its future discounted cash flows. But because we have no way to forecast cash flows into the distant future, some argue that the EMH is an empty idea.

The EMH is the concept that has raised perhaps the most debate after recent market crises, including the 2007–09 crisis. It is an academic hypothesis that markets are "efficient" in the sense that market prices are always equal to theoretical prices. But it seems to be at odds with the reality of a market that lost 57% of its value from its peak in October 2007 to its bottom in March 2009 and then bounced back to its precrash high within four years.

The twin hypotheses of asset pricing and the EMH are not verifiable.

Risk Measurement and Risk Management

Risk management, too, was in for criticism following the recent financial crisis. It is not the *concept* of risk management that is questioned, however, but our tools and what we measure. First, the adequacy of our risk measurements and models is questioned. For example, most asset management firms still use measurements based on the assumption of normality, such as the risk metric VaR. Second, the scope of risk management may be too narrow. In particular, the tools fail to take into consideration systemic risk—a key failure in light of the wide use of derivative products that can propagate risk in ways that are difficult to understand and control.

Mainstream theory maintains that the economy and markets are in a state of general equilibrium and that only large, unpredictable exogenous events can disturb this equilibrium. Attempts to explain crises that are not explained by mainstream theory have taken two approaches. One approach starts with the observation that economies and financial markets are unstable complex systems. Far from being self-correcting equilibrium systems, economies and financial markets have endogenous mechanisms that may lead to a crisis when many interacting units (e.g., financial institutions) form networks in which very large connected components occur. A high density of connections can lead to cascading effects. Researchers working in this field apply complex system theory to identify potentially dangerous thresholds of connectivity.

The other approach goes back to Hyman Minsky, who maintained in his financial instability hypothesis that crises are generated by an excess of money, which fuels speculation and causes asset price inflation, followed by debt deflation.[7] Researchers attempting to model bubbles and crashes following Minsky's hypothesis are applying tools from nonlinear dynamics.

Teaching Finance: Can We Do Better?

Should the recent financial crisis, which contradicted so many central "truths" of modern economic and finance theory, change how we teach investment management? What should we be telling students about our theories and our models? Do we need to teach a new investment paradigm, as some have argued? What do we include in and what do we exclude from the curriculum of students whose objective is to manage other people's money? And has anything changed since the start of the 2007–09 financial crisis?

The overall perception of the academics and practitioners we surveyed is that not much has changed to date. Two reasons are given: First, not everyone is persuaded that changes are called for. Many academics believe that the current framework is solid and that we need only make minor adjustments. Second, some academics believe that throwing 40 years of research out of the curriculum straightaway is not so easy. These academics are trying to gradually rebalance their approach to teaching finance and the curriculum.

Given the widespread criticism of mainstream finance theory based on an idealization of markets, however, we ask: If our financial economics and finance theory are indeed of little practical use, in that they do not describe market reality, is it appropriate to teach the theory to students who, for the most part, are in school for practical purposes? And if the practical applicability of mainstream theory is so poor, why teach the difficult mathematics in which the ideas of general equilibrium, market efficiency, modern portfolio theory, and continuous-time asset pricing are cast?

Those in favor of keeping our theory argue that, although the theory is imperfect (it is still a work in progress), it is the *way* we teach the theory (too simplistic) that needs to change. Most (not all) sources we interviewed in our study agree that today's theory provides a useful framework for thinking about economic and finance problems but

[7]See Hyman P. Minsky, *Stabilizing an Unstable Economy* (New Haven, CT: Yale University Press, 1986) and "The Financial Instability Hypothesis," Working Paper No. 74, Jerome Levy Economics Institute of Bard College (May 1992).

has limitations. Because today's finance theory has limitations, many suggest that it be taught less dogmatically, more pragmatically, than it is currently taught.

What specifically should we do in terms of changing the way we teach finance theory—in particular, the way we teach finance to students aspiring to be investment professionals?

Consider general equilibrium theory, which states that the economy and markets are in a state of general equilibrium, meaning that the market for every good and service clears at a price where the quantity supplied equals the quantity demanded; this equilibrium can be disturbed only by large unpredictable exogenous events. The recurrence of financial crises led David Romer at the University of California, Berkeley, to conclude, however, that financial shocks are more commonplace than exceptional. Some believe that because financial markets are essentially nonstationary and unstable, we are neither teaching the right concepts nor giving the appropriate tools to future investment managers.

For example, diversification is widely held to be a sound probabilistic concept, but the benefits of diversification may change as market states, correlations, or expected returns change. In the case of market corrections or crashes, even a well-diversified portfolio is not protected against large losses. Students are taught about diversification, but they are not taught what might be done when the correlations among markets grow and diversification does not work—or works less well than it has been working. Nor are students taught how to deal with chaos or non-normal distributions, which is another illustration of the fact that we are not preparing students to handle events outside the theory of general equilibrium. In teaching diversification, we would benefit students if we talked about structural breaks and estimation errors of the variance–covariance matrix and their implications for the composition of efficient portfolios and if we focused on how to reduce estimation error, account for fat-tail correlations, and perform extreme-event stress testing.

Another theory, the CAPM, is a flawed partial equilibrium theory, and the one-factor model is sloppy econometrics. Yet, despite the fact that the tenets of the CAPM have been invalidated in numerous empirical studies, the model is still widely taught as a theoretical framework for asset pricing. Should we continue to teach the CAPM?

The academic emphasis on asset-pricing models, which focus on precise asset pricing as opposed to pragmatic decision making, has also been questioned. The argument here is that asset pricing is an intellectual exercise; focusing on decision making forces one to think pragmatically and gives priority to forecasting and uncertainty.

Some practitioners and academics believe there is an overdependence on a theoretical framework that does not describe real markets. They seek empirical verification and are in search of a different type of theory, one that is more in line with the paradigm of the physical sciences and thus of more practical use. For example, Andrew Ang, professor of business at Columbia Business School, considers factor theory central to asset management. He believes that understanding factors is the key to understanding returns.

That the reality of markets should be the primary object of study is perhaps the key adjustment that needs to be made to both the theory and the teaching of finance.

Finally, risk measures commonly used in asset management, such as standard deviation and VaR, have come under criticism for their inadequacies—particularly because of their reliance on the assumption of a normal distribution. These commonly used measures are considered too narrow in scope because they are typically limited to a statistical measurement of market risk. The focus on market risk measurement is questioned: Most of the literature and especially investment texts have focused on *equity markets* and two-tailed risk, even though the largest collapses of the last two decades or so (the failure of Long-Term Capital Management and the subprime mortgage crisis) occurred in the fixed-income markets. In short, not enough attention is being paid to credit risk evaluation, collapse models, and cross-market contagion.

What about market crashes? The potential impact of a crisis on a portfolio can be enormous. Crises occur, but they do not find their place in mainstream finance's general equilibrium theory. Perhaps these events should be factored into the risk structure.

What's Missing in the Curricula for Future Investment Professionals?

We asked academics and practitioners what, in the wake of the most recent financial crisis, needs to be reinforced or (re)introduced in programs preparing students for jobs in investment management.

Clearly, to pack additional courses into the typical two-year MBA finance program would not be easy. Another problem in discussing the curriculum is the diversity of roles. Is there any common body of knowledge that should be shared among market participants and, therefore, reflected in the curriculum? Yet another problem is today's emphasis on theories and models not based on empirical evidence.

As for PhD programs in finance, the main concern is that too much time is allotted to mastering difficult mathematical methods at the expense of developing broad knowledge of economics and finance.

Clearly, any educational program is a compromise between time constraints and a potentially long series of topics to cover. Here is the list of subjects (in order of number of mentions) that our sources believe should be reinforced in or (re)introduced to the curriculum:

- macroeconomics, including a historical perspective on macroeconomics,
- the history of financial markets and economic history,
- behavioral finance,
- statistics beyond the use of the normal distribution,
- risk management, and
- ethics.

The current interest in macroeconomics and its history is probably a reaction to the recent financial crisis, which (unduly) surprised so many academics and market participants. Despite its importance, macroeconomics—not any particular approach or ideology—is widely considered to be poorly covered in current curricula. Rather than the formalism and mathematics of the general equilibrium theory, or anomalies in capital markets, what would be beneficial to students is more exposure to macroeconomics and its related fields, such as interest rates, exchange rates, and inflation. Many of our sources believe that a mix of judgment and nonquantitative macro/markets analysis is required to identify regularities and patterns in events and to recognize regime shifts.

There are two other compelling reasons for reinforcing macroeconomics in the curriculum. First, in the end, the economy drives financial markets. A disconnect between economies and financial markets generally implies that financial profits are being created artificially, thus bringing about a situation of instability. Second, in the wake of the 2007–09 financial crisis and ensuing Great Recession, governments are playing a growing role in the economy and markets.

Another important subject frequently mentioned as missing from the curricula for future investment professionals is the history of finance and of financial markets. The 2007–09 financial crisis alerted many to the role of history as a measure and model of crises. Teaching the history of finance and of financial markets would give students a long-term perspective, allow them to learn from past crises, and provide illustrations of, for example, the effect of financial euphoria on markets. It would also provide a way of testing our conventional hypotheses.

In addition to history, learning from current affairs (in particular, with regard to the recent crisis) was singled out by our sources as an oft-neglected area.

The need to include more on behavioral finance in the curriculum for future investment professionals was also noted. Behavioral finance began to move into finance programs even before the 2002 Nobel Prize in Economics was awarded to the behavioral psychologist and economist Daniel Kahneman. The objective of behavioral finance is to improve our understanding of markets and our forecasts by attempting to explain market movements as the result of cognitive biases (deviations from so-called rational judgment) on the part of market participants. How do we teach behavioral finance? What do we expect to be able to do with it?

The increasing relevance of statistics, mathematics, and modeling in finance programs arises from the greater availability of market and economic data and low-cost computing power. The issue of teaching these subjects to future investment professionals has two sides: Some curricula put too much emphasis on statistics, mathematics, and modeling, so students risk losing the big macroeconomic picture; others do not teach enough statistics, mathematics, and modeling, so students receive insufficient training and are unable to work with large datasets, apply the appropriate modeling techniques, and interpret the results. Learning how to collect and evaluate data (skills not always taught by the school), as well as how to create models (if only with simple modeling methods), should be part of every finance student's formal education.

Finally, with respect to risk management, portfolio management is based on the notion of optimizing the risk–reward trade-off. Risk management, therefore, is at the heart of asset management. But although things have begun to change since the 2007–09 financial crisis, many believe that risk management is not sufficiently taught in most finance programs. Risk management entails more than risk–return optimization. First, as proposed by Benoit Mandelbrot more than 50 years ago, the notion of portfolio risk should be based on non-normal (as opposed to normal) distributions.[8] Second, accounting is an important source of risk that deserves more attention in curricula than it has been receiving. Third, risk management is asset/liability management, not asset management alone. The role of liabilities and the interaction between assets and liabilities are not well covered in business schools, except in the few insurance programs that exist. The "meta-risk" of model failure and systemic risk are other categories of risk that have been given little consideration in most risk management curricula.

Landing a Job in Investment Management

In the recruitment of recent graduates for jobs in investment management, the emphasis is now being placed on solid economic reasoning and understanding of the "big picture," including the global macro and (geo)political situations. The growing importance of good macroeconomic reasoning represents something of a change from recent years. Firms, including quantitative asset management firms, are now looking for economic reasoning skills *and* math in the same person. Moreover, they are apparently having difficulty finding that combination of attributes. From the point of view of business

[8]Benoit Mandelbrot, "The Variation of Certain Speculative Prices," *Journal of Business*, vol. 36, no. 4 (October 1963):394–419.

schools and universities preparing students (including PhDs) for jobs in investment management, this trend calls for a well-rounded curriculum that encompasses a broad spectrum of fundamental knowledge and quantitative skills.

One criticism of most current finance programs is that too little attention is paid to creativity and out-of-the-box thinking in developing students' ability to understand, to critique, and to find new angles to a problem. Students need to be exposed to various ideas and points of view in order to develop the mental flexibility that is required to think outside of established schemas. Many human resources managers find these qualities lacking in graduates coming from traditional business schools that teach (often dogmatically) mainstream economic and finance theory.

In addition, many finance programs, especially mathematical finance programs, are criticized for putting too much emphasis on models. The criticism is that these programs are divorced from events in the real world and produce recruits who have an equation for everything but who lack broader knowledge.

According to human resources managers, although the school does count, recruitment is a question of the individual. Business school graduates with an MBA are typically "top picks" in the United States. The situation is different in Europe, where some report that they have seen negative added value in MBA hires. That is, the cost of recruits from these programs is high, and the value they add is not sufficient to cover the cost.

The complete audiobook can be found at
www.cfapubs.org/toc/rf/2014/2014/3.

Use your mobile device to scan the QR code to go straight to the webpage.

FUNDAMENTAL VALUE IS A LONG-TERM CONCEPT (A SUMMARY)

Brian Singer, CFA
Keynote presentation given 15 June 2015 at CFA Society Minnesota, Minneapolis
Summary prepared by Laurence B. Siegel

Understanding fundamental value is necessary but not sufficient for being a successful investor. When I got my CFA charter in the 1980s, there were not as many people trained in what fundamental value is. Now, there are hundreds of thousands.

How many people here have read "I, Pencil" by Leonard Read? The essence of Read's essay is there is not a single person in the world who knows how to make a pencil;

Video of Brian Singer's Keynote Presentation

Watch the video at www.cfainstitute.org/keynote

making one involves coordination of dozens of mining and manufacturing processes all over the world.

Now think about the assumptions underlying modern portfolio theory (MPT): The world is static, and everybody has all the relevant information. They all interpret it in the same way, without lags, errors, or biases. Yet, this is in the same world where no one knows how to make a pencil!

There is something inconsistent between MPT and this reality. MPT is a single-period concept, and in that regard, it is static. But equilibrium is not static. A static equilibrium is a ball rolling to the bottom of a bowl and staying there. A better way to think about the world we live in is "complex adaptive equilibrium," a plate with little dimples. The ball may rest in one, but with a little jostling, it will go rest in another one. Multiple equilibria can exist at any one time, and which equilibrium you are in is path dependent, sensitive to initial conditions, and complex in other ways.

Let's apply this concept to fund selection. Let's say you provide your client with a 10% long-run annualized return; that is good, but if the first return is –90%, the client will not be with you. The world is nonlinear and is characterized by "endogenous novelty." Flows in and out of funds are explained by differentiation, selection, and amplification. Differentiation amounts to managers trying different approaches, such as the January effect, a Fama–French–Carhart four-factor model, smart beta, or evolving alpha. Things that are tried and work well are selected. Because the success attracts more money to the same securities as those that produced the effect in the first place, the effect is amplified until it goes away or reverses.

We also underestimate the amount of change that can take place over a long period. I was reading, for fun, the history of wages from US Colonial times to 1928. One of the jobs was "vamper maker." (A vamper is a part of a shoe.) There were only four textiles: cotton, silk, woolens, and hosiery/underwear. All of the jobs from before 1928 have been competed away, as have most of the products.

Both traditional valuation and complex systems apply in our world of investing.

Fundamental value is a powerful concept. It is the equilibrium price; it is what you would be willing to pay for a package of cash flows, given the undiversifiable risk that it introduces into a portfolio. But it is a very long-term concept, not one that applies when you are negotiating prices under stress or unusual conditions. It is relevant in the sense that prices converge on fundamental value over an 8 to 10-year period; it is a gravitational force pulling price toward value, dynamically and very slowly. We have to navigate the erratic paths that prices take toward fundamental value because we live in a dynamic world with multiple equilibria. Evaluating the CAPM alpha of a stock or portfolio based on daily returns is very naive.

So, as an investor, what we are trained to do in a generalist, CFA Program–type curriculum is to calculate this fundamental value. Maybe that was necessary and sufficient 25 years ago, but now, markets and the environment are more complex. To learn more about how complexity is increasing and affects markets, refer to the works of W. Brian Arthur (Santa Fe Institute); Didier Sornette, a physicist who has turned his attention to markets; and Eric Beinhocker (Institute for New Economic Thinking, University of Oxford), whose *The Origin of Wealth* is a good introduction.

If you graph the S&P 500 Index in real terms going back a little more than 100 years, you see that the first half of the past century had a slower rate of growth; the second half was faster, and we do not know about this new century yet. Now, why would the second half of the 20th century be unique? (Audience: "It was peaceful.") Are you kidding? The Cold War, mutually assured destruction, was peaceful? Well, actually, it was. But now we live in a period of geopolitical instability, just like the first half of the past century was. What else was unique in the fast-growing period? The baby boom and labor force growth. These are the types of things we can think about to understand fundamental value.

Note that real global growth averaged 3.5% before the global financial crisis; what do you think it was after the crisis? Surprise... it was 3.5%, and probably will be for the next half century. (Most of the pre-crisis growth was in the developed world; most of the post-crisis growth, in the developing.)

I cannot pick stocks; I am a macro, top-down investor. But most top-down investors rely on economic forecasts. Let's see whether they help or not. I got Angus Maddison's GDP growth data back to 1871. There is no relationship with the stock market—that is, the correlation was zero over one-, two-, three-, four-year, and even longer periods. Even though the assets are claims on the underlying economic engine, the statistical relationship takes longer than that to show up. With non-overlapping 20-year periods you do get correlation. The variables (GDP and stock market) are cointegrated.

What does it mean to say the variables are cointegrated? Consider a man and his puppy. The man is drunk, and he is wandering around in a park at night—random, Brownian motion. From a distance, an observer would say that the man's and the puppy's movements are uncorrelated, because a random walk is uncorrelated to everything. But knowing that the puppy belongs to the man, you realize that the best place to look for the man is near his puppy! There is a relationship between the two "assets." The two sets of movements are not correlated in the short run, but they are cointegrated, like economic growth and the stock market.

So, to make money in markets, you need very long-range forecasts, not just a few quarters or years. The fundamental value of equities moves up at about the equity cost of capital (long-run expected return) every year. From information about fundamental values, we can estimate future long-run returns. For US equities the long-run expected nominal return is about 4%, implying that these equities are a little expensive. The corresponding numbers are 7.5% and 11% for developed non-US and emerging market equities, respectively. So, the opportunity is outside the United States.

Bonds are not providing great opportunities on a fundamental basis. But would you short bonds today? Bond yields are a manipulated rate that could continue to be manipulated for some time to come. Knowing that yields are too low does not tell you what to do. The bond market is a complex system, and fundamental value does not apply over the relevant time frame.

VI. WORKSHOP FOR THE PRACTITIONER SUMMARIES

14TH ANNUAL WORKSHOP FOR THE PRACTITIONER

Presentations at the 14th Annual Research for the Practitioner Workshop, 26 April 2015

For the past 14 years, the CFA Institute Research Foundation has held a Workshop for the Practitioner on the Sunday afternoon of the CFA Institute Annual Conference. The event is designed to showcase important topics in investment management and is free to all conference attendees.

In recent years, the workshop has addressed such topics as manager selection, managing tail risk, and factor analysis. In 2015, speaker Pippa Malmgren discussed the geopolitics of investing and Joachim Klement, CFA, discussed investor risk profiling—both topics supported by the Research Foundation (a complete summary of their work is available earlier in this review).

Abstracts and video for the content presented during the 2015 workshop follow.

Speaker Pippa Malmgren: *Geopolitics for Investors*

Geopolitical issues have a profound effect on investment strategies and results. Investors inevitably must balance risk and reward. Geopolitics can bring both risks and opportunities, large and small, onto the investment landscape. The question is, How much time and effort can be devoted to this particular task? Prediction is nearly impossible, but preparedness is attainable and desirable. Fund managers and investors need to ask whether preparedness is best achieved through scenario planning, by including geopolitics as one of many drivers of the investment strategy, or by changing the investment team or the information sources and services that the team uses. As always, markets represent diverse interests and abilities. Some investors will find a way to add geopolitics to their investment scenarios and to profit from it. Others will take comfort in knowing that they were not alone in utterly ignoring geopolitics. This monograph offers some core ideas about how to think about the subject. These ideas may prove useful as geopolitics returns to the investment landscape with increasing force.

Video of Pippa Malmgren's Workshop Presentation

Watch the video at www.cfainstitute.org/malmgren

Speaker Joachim Klement: *Investor Risk Profiling: An Overview*

The current standard process of risk profiling through questionnaires is highly unreliable and typically explains less than 15% of the variation in risky assets between investors—mostly because the questionnaires focus on socio-economic variables and hypothetical scenarios. The existing research in risk profiling shows, however, that several factors can provide more accurate and reliable insights into the risk profile of investors. Among these factors are the lifetime experiences an investor has had, the financial decisions made in the past, and the influence of family and friends as well as advisers. By using these factors, practitioners can get a better understanding of their clients' preferences in order to recommend suitable investment strategies and products.

Video of Joachim Klement's Workshop Presentation

Watch the video at www.cfainstitute.org/klement

VII. 50TH ANNIVERSARY FORUM

Photo credit: Alan Barnett.

Research Foundation Vice Chair Joachim Klement, CFA, introduces the RF 50th anniversary event.

INTRODUCTION TO THE FORUM

The CFA Institute Research Foundation 50th Anniversary Forum was held at the New York Society of Security Analysts (NYSSA) in 2015. The event featured two panel discussions and the granting of the James R. Vertin Award.

Photo credit: Alan Barnett.

RF 50th Anniversary Forum panelists Joachim Klement, CFA, Stephen J. Brown, and Jason C. Hsu (left to right) compare notes before the big event.

EVOLUTION OF INVESTMENT RESEARCH

Moderator: Larry Siegel (RF research director)

Participants:

Stephen J. Brown (New York University and *Financial Analysts Journal* executive editor)

Jason C. Hsu (Research Affiliates and RF Board)

Joachim Klement, CFA (Wellershoff & Partners Ltd. and RF Board)

Panelists discussed

- the importance of the Uniform Prudent Investor Act and the impact of the financial crisis,
- the effect of competition on market efficiency and fees and the impact that differentiation is having in the marketplace, and
- the move toward a bifurcated market with low-cost indexing and high-cost very active differentiated products.

Video of Evolution of Investment Research Forum

Watch the video at www.cfainstitute.org/RFmultimedia

RF 50th Anniversary Forum moderator and RF Research Director Larry Siegel (far right) talks about the future of the investment profession with panelists Stephen J. Brown, Jason C. Hsu, and Joachim Klement, CFA (left to right).

HELPING THE INVESTMENT PROFESSION

Moderator: Jason Zweig (United States—*Wall Street Journal*)

Participants:

Ted Aronson, CFA (United States—Aronson Johnson Ortiz)

Vikram Kuriyan, CFA (India—Indian School of Business and RF Board)

Fred Lebel, CFA (Switzerland—Hedge Fund Selections/OFI MGA and CFA Institute Board of Governors)

Paul Smith, CFA (Hong Kong—CFA Institute and RF Board)

Panelists discussed

- Should we move from managing investments to managing investors?
- How close is the investment management business to becoming a profession?
- How will regulation affect the investment management business?

Video of Helping the Investment Profession Forum

Watch the video at www.cfainstitute.org/RFmultimedia

CFA Institute CEO Paul Smith, CFA (far right), participating in the RF panel with Ted Aronson, CFA, Fred Lebel, CFA, and moderator Jason Zweig (left to right).

RF 50th Anniversary Forum moderator Jason Zweig (far right) with other attendees reviewing Research Foundation books.

Photo credit: Alan Barnett.

Allison Adams (right)—head, communications and content strategy at CFA Institute—talks to Jason Zweig (left) during the RF 50th Anniversary Forum.

PRESENTATION UPON RECEIVING THE JAMES R. VERTIN AWARD

Frank J. Fabozzi, CFA

In early 1971, I began my university teaching career. After a few years, I was given the opportunity to teach an undergraduate investment management course. Fundamentally, I taught modern portfolio theory and asset-pricing theory from a theoretical perspective. That is a nice way of saying that I taught out of the popular textbooks at the time, ignoring the realities of the real world and implementation issues and without focusing on the consumer of financial services. So an apt description of my teaching approach was that I was a "textbook professor." Finance majors at the time felt comfortable with this approach given, but today, students correctly complain about instructors who fail to link theory and practice.

Video of Frank Fabozzi's Presentation

Watch the video at www.cfainstitute.org/RFmultimedia

Photo credit: Alan Barnett.

Frank Fabozzi, CFA, gives his acceptance speech for the Vertin Award.

I soon came to realize that to be a more effective instructor, I needed to close the gap between theory and practice. Collecting my mail from my department's mailroom one day in 1974, I noticed a flier on the floor adjacent to a trash basket, apparently tossed away by a colleague whose ability to toss an item into a basket rivaled Shaquille O'Neal's free-throw skills. Fortunately, that miscue had a major impact on my career.

The flier was for an upstart journal, the *Journal of Portfolio Management*, edited by a prominent economist, Peter Bernstein, author of numerous best-selling books on various economic issues. The inaugural issue included prominent economists and asset managers—Paul Samuelson; Fischer Black; Dean LeBaron, CFA; Wayne Wagner; and Keith Ambachtsheer. The lead article, "The State of the Art in Our Profession," was by James Vertin, CFA.

The title of the article seemed precisely like the type of work I needed to read to bridge the theory–practice gap. The price of receiving the inaugural issue was the optimal consumer price: free. So I requested a complimentary copy. The issue was all that I hoped for and more. In fact, in the 40th anniversary issue of the journal, John Bogle, founder of Vanguard, credited the article by Paul Samuelson in the inaugural issue, "Challenge to Judgment," as having a major influence in launching an index fund. But let's return to the article by James Vertin. Not only was the message helpful to me in closing the theory–practice gap and the impediments to the use of "modern investment theory" at that time, but also, if read today, it conveys a message that is equally applicable.

Given the practitioner-oriented articles in the journal's inaugural issue, I became an avid reader of the journal, encouraging students to read it. In the 5th anniversary issue of the journal (and also commemorating the 50th anniversary of the 1929 market crash), another insightful article authored by James Vertin appeared, "What Can the Future Tell Us about the Past?"

It was not until 1978 that I mustered enough courage to submit a paper to the journal. The paper, "Quality of Earnings: A Test of Market Efficiency," resulted in an ongoing dialogue with Peter about the empirical evidence challenging the efficient market hypothesis. In the summer of 1983, Peter invited me to lunch in New York City. The agenda was to discuss my interest in becoming the managing editor of the *Journal of Portfolio Management* for a few years and then taking over as editor with total editorial control. In 1985, Peter handed me the reins of the journal, and I have held them since. All of this starting because a colleague failed to sink a basket with a flier!

Photo credit: Alan Barnett.

Vertin Award winner Frank Fabozzi, CFA (left), recognizes frequent coauthor Sergio Focardi for his contributions to investment research.

Group picture of NYSSA, CFA Institute, and Research Foundation board members with Vertin Award winner Frank Fabozzi, CFA.

VIII. AWARDS AND RECOGNITION

JAMES R. VERTIN AWARD

The James R. Vertin Award is presented periodically to recognize individuals who have produced a body of research notable for its relevance and enduring value to investment professionals. This award was established in 1996 to honor James R. Vertin, CFA, for his outstanding leadership in promoting excellence and relevancy in research and education.

RF Research Committee Chair Wayne Wagner (left) presents the Vertin Award to Frank Fabozzi, CFA (right).

2015 Vertin Award Winner

Frank J. Fabozzi, CFA

Frank J. Fabozzi, CFA, is a professor of finance at EDHEC Business School, France, and a member of the EDHEC Risk Institute. Prior to joining EDHEC, he held various professorial positions in finance at Yale and Massachusetts Institute of Technology. Professor Fabozzi also served as James Wei Visiting Professor in Entrepreneurship at Princeton University, where he is also currently a research fellow in the Department of Operations Research and Financial Engineering. A trustee for the BlackRock family of closed-end funds and the equity-liquidity complexes, Fabozzi has authored and edited many books on asset management. He is the recipient of the C. Stewart Sheppard Award from CFA Institute, and in 2002, he was inducted into the Fixed Income Analysts Society Hall of Fame. Fabozzi received his bachelor's and master's degrees in economics and statistics from the City College of New York and his PhD in economics from the City University of New York.

Video of Frank Fabozzi Vertin Award Interview

Watch the video at www.cfainstitute.org/fabozzi

Past Vertin Award Winners

2014 Kenneth R. French

2013 Richard C. Grinold

2013 Ronald N. Kahn

2012 Elroy Dimson

2010 Roger Clarke

2009 Robert Shiller

2008 Keith Ambachtsheer

2007 Campbell R. Harvey

2006 Clifford S. Asness

2005 Andrew W. Lo

2004 Edwin J. Elton

2004 Martin Gruber

2003 Barr Rosenberg

2002 William L. Fouse, CFA

2001 Rex A. Sinquefield

2001 Roger G. Ibbotson

2000 Peter L. Bernstein

1998 Martin L. Leibowitz

1997 Jack L. Treynor

1996 William F. Sharpe

RESEARCH FOUNDATION SOCIETY AWARD

The Research Foundation Society Award is an annual award to the CFA Institute member society or societies that do the best job of using Research Foundation (RF) content in an activity, product, or service. The goal of the award is to build a strong, effective working relationship between societies and the Research Foundation.

2015 RF Society Award winners at the CFA Institute Society Leadership Conference in Hong Kong.

Some current RF programs that have evolved out of the Research Foundation Society Award include the following:

- RF content in society newsletters and on society websites
- RF author events and RF book distribution
- RF content distributed in company, university, and regulator outreach efforts
- RF content translations and creation of a book club with author conference call
- RF Research Challenge adviser presentation and RF book distribution
- RF board meeting hosting and creation of a society library with RF books

Congratulations to the 2015 Research Foundation Society Award winners

- CFA Society Cleveland
- CFA Society Finland
- CFA Society France
- CFA Society Los Angeles
- CFA Society Milwaukee
- CFA Society Pakistan
- CFA Society Sydney

And congratulations to the societies that have won this award in the past:

2014 award winners

- CFA China
- CFA Society San Francisco
- Indian Association of Investment Professionals
- CFA Society Philadelphia (Encouragement Award[1])

2013 award winners

- CFA Society Barbados
- CFA Society Hawaii
- CFA Society Pakistan
- CFA Society Italy
- CFA Society Emirates
- CFA Society Toronto
- CFA Society France (Encouragement Award)

[1]The Encouragement Award is granted to a society whose efforts with the Research Foundation are commendable but not quite extensive enough to receive the Society Award.

2012 award winners

- Boston Security Analysts Society
- CFA Society Argentina & Uruguay
- CFA Society Buffalo
- CFA Society Bulgaria
- CFA Society Rochester
- CFA Society Seattle

The Research Foundation also extends a special thanks to societies that have hosted, or will be hosting, our trustee board meetings:

- CFA Society Toronto (Spring 2013)
- CFA Society San Francisco (Fall 2013)
- CFA Society Los Angeles (Spring 2014)
- CFA Society Minnesota (Spring 2015)
- New York Society of Security Analysts (Fall 2015)
- CFA Society Dallas/Fort Worth (Spring 2016)
- CFA Montréal (Fall 2016)
- CFA Society United Kingdom (Spring 2017)

RESEARCH FOUNDATION LEADERSHIP CIRCLE

The Research Foundation Leadership Circle honors investment professionals whose outstanding commitment and contributions have benefited the Research Foundation over an extended period of time. The Research Foundation is honored to recognize the following members of the Leadership Circle:

Gary Brinson, CFA

George Noyes, CFA

Frank Reilly, CFA

Fred Speece, CFA

Walter Stern, CFA

James R. Vertin, CFA

IX. PAST AND FUTURE PUBLICATIONS

RECENT PUBLICATIONS FROM THE RESEARCH FOUNDATION ARCHIVE

2014

Monographs

The New Economics of Liquidity and Financial Frictions (December)
David Adler

> *The New Economics of Liquidity and Financial Frictions* is a book about a new branch of economics that is largely a synthesis of macro and finance. In many ways, it is a radical departure from the older, frictionless approach still prevalent in economic textbooks and most of academia. This book provides a new understanding and approach to asset pricing, risk measurement and management, central banking policy, and the overall working of today's economy, including questions of financial stability.

Investment Management: A Science to Teach or an Art to Learn? (May)
Frank J. Fabozzi, CFA, Sergio M. Focardi, and Caroline Jonas

> Following the 2007–09 financial crisis, mainstream finance theory was criticized for failing to forecast the market crash, which resulted in large losses for investors. Has our finance theory, which many consider an idealization that does not take reality into account, failed investors? Do we need to reconsider the theory and how it is taught (and practiced)? This book explores current critiques of mainstream theory and discusses implications for the curricula of finance programs as well as for practitioners. In so doing, the authors integrate a review of the literature supported by conversations with finance professors, asset managers, and other market players.

Environmental Markets: A New Asset Class (January)
Richard L. Sandor, Nathan J. Clark, Murali Kanakasabai, and Rafael L. Marques

Population growth, industrialization, and urbanization in the past 200 years have resulted in local, national, and global pollution of our environment. Markets, when designed properly, can be a powerful agent to combat this pollution. Environmental finance is thus the art and science of using economic incentives, financial tools, and market mechanisms to achieve desired environmental outcomes.

Literature Reviews

"Islamic Finance: Ethics, Concepts, Practice" (November)
Usman Hayat, CFA, and Adeel Malik, PhD

Islamic economic thought and finance are rooted in Islamic ethics. Their ideals and means are not, however, exclusive to Islam. The principles of Islamic finance emphasize market-based risk-sharing modes of financing that promote assets and enterprise, deploy finance in service of the real economy, and facilitate redistribution of wealth and opportunity. Modern Islamic financial practices, however, privilege legal form over economic substance, which creates an expectations gap between Islamic finance's theory and practice. In the wake of the global financial crisis of 2007–2008, the ideas underlying Islamic finance appeal to those more concerned with the broader impact of finance on society.

"Investment Professionals and Fiduciary Duties" (September)
Marianne M. Jennings

The distinction between brokers and investment advisers has become increasingly blurred over the past 30 years. In a 2011 study, the US SEC recommended that there be one uniform standard for both broker/dealers and investment advisers. In addition, all investment professionals could benefit from some standards. Through a review of market history, literature, and general principles from fiduciary relationships, some simple concepts emerge that could help investment professionals navigate the conflicts of interest that are inevitable given the often blended roles that they play in the financial markets.

"The Principal–Agent Problem in Finance" (March)
Sunit N. Shah

The relationship between a principal and the agent who acts on the principal's behalf contains the potential for conflicts of interest. The principal–agent problem arises when this relationship involves both misaligned incentives and information asymmetry. In asset management, factors contributing to the principal–agent problem include managers' compensation structures and investors' tendency to focus on short-term performance. In the banking industry, myriad principal–agent relationships and complex instruments provide a fertile breeding ground for incentive conflicts, many of which were highlighted by the recent financial crisis.

2013

Monographs

Manager Selection (December)
Scott D. Stewart, CFA

Manager selection is a critical step in implementing any investment program. Investors hire portfolio managers to act as their agents, and portfolio managers are then expected to perform to the best of their abilities and in the investors' best interests. Investors must practice due diligence when selecting portfolio managers. They need to not only identify skillful managers but also determine the appropriate weights to assign to those managers. This book is designed to help investors improve their ability to select managers. Achieving this goal includes reviewing techniques for hiring active, indexed, and alternative managers; highlighting strategies for setting portfolio manager weights and monitoring current managers; and considering the value of quantitative and qualitative methods for successful manager selection.

Fundamentals of Futures and Options (November)
Roger G. Clarke, Harindra de Silva, CFA, and Steven Thorley, CFA

Derivative securities and markets have experienced tremendous worldwide growth since 1970. But even so, they are not always well understood. To remedy this situation, the authors explain the link between options and futures and the underlying security or index from which they ultimately derive their value. Pricing and hedging relationships of futures contracts, option characteristics and strategies, and option pricing and hedging relationships are also addressed. To further assist the reader, the authors include exercises to reinforce the concepts as well as a glossary. The result is an updated look at options and futures that can benefit many of us.

Life Annuities: An Optimal Product for Retirement Income (May)
Moshe A. Milevsky

This book provides a summary of research on life annuities, longevity insurance, and their role in the "optimal" retirement portfolio. It starts with an overview of institutional aspects, moves on to discuss valuation issues, and concludes with a comprehensive review of the scholarly literature.

Literature Reviews

"The Evolution of Asset/Liability Management" (September)
Ronald J. Ryan, CFA

This review tracks the development of asset/liability management from its roots in liability management outsourcing to its most recent interpretation as a broad liability-driven investing strategy.

"Ethics and Financial Markets: The Role of the Analyst" (September)
Marianne M. Jennings

The ethical issues that financial professionals face are no different from the ethical issues in any profession—or, indeed, the day-to-day dilemmas we all face. These issues are readily resolved through the use of three simple questions: Does this violate the law? Is this honest? What if I were on the other side? These three basic ethical standards are often complicated, extrapolated, rationalized, refined, and confused as those in the financial markets grapple with what they believe are more complex ethical issues today than in the past. But as this review shows, the ethical issues in the financial markets today are no different from those that managers of money and assets, financial advisers, and analysts have faced over the centuries.

2012

Monographs

A New Look at Currency Investing (December)
Momtchil Pojarliev, CFA, and Richard M. Levich

The authors of this book examine the rationale for investing in currency. They highlight several features of currency returns that make currency an attractive asset class for institutional investors. Using style factors to model currency returns provides a natural way to decompose returns into alpha and beta components. They find that several established currency trading strategies (variants of carry, trend-following, and value strategies) produce consistent returns that can be proxied as style or risk factors and have the nature of beta returns. Then, using two datasets of returns of actual currency hedge funds, they find that some currency managers produce true alpha. Finally, they find that adding to an institutional investor's portfolio even a small amount of currency exposure—particularly to alpha generators—can make a meaningful positive impact on the portfolio's performance.

Life-Cycle Investing: Financial Education and Consumer Protection (November)
Edited by Zvi Bodie, Laurence B. Siegel, and Lisa Stanton, CFA

Third in the series of Boston University–sponsored conferences titled "The Future of Life-Cycle Saving and Investing," the May 2011 conference again brought together academic researchers, educators, advisers, and regulators. This time, we analyzed the gaps in consumers' current financial knowledge, how those gaps might be narrowed through financial education programs, and how consumer protection regarding financial products might be strengthened—with a focus on low- and middle-income households. Although there was general agreement that consumers of financial products and services make many costly mistakes, there was also considerable disagreement about relying primarily on consumer financial education programs to correct those mistakes.

Fund Management: An Emotional Finance Perspective (August)
David Tuckett and Richard J. Taffler

To increase understanding of the real world of the fund manager, the authors apply principles from emotional finance. They report their findings from analysing in-depth interviews of 52 traditional and quantitative-oriented equity managers. In particular, they examine the importance of storytelling in the managers' ability to act in the face of uncertainty. The nature of the fund managers' job requires them to cope with emotions that, particularly if denied, can threaten to overwhelm their thinking.

Expected Returns on Major Asset Classes (June)
Antti Ilmanen

Can the art and science of investment management be reduced to a set of patterns that markets generally follow, in apparent violation of the efficient market hypothesis? Can investors reasonably expect to make money from the knowledge of these patterns, even after they have not only been identified but also widely exploited? Although one's first guess might be that the answers to these questions are no, at least sometimes, the answer is yes.

Literature Reviews

"The New Field of Liquidity and Financial Frictions" (June)
David Adler

Illiquidity and other financial frictions are critical to financial markets and the overall economy. This literature review provides a synopsis of academic research in this rapidly developing specialty field, offering insights into liquidity and asset pricing, systemic risk, macro frictions, and new models of the causes of a liquidity crisis.

"Equity Valuation and Inflation: A Review" (January)
Stephen E. Wilcox, CFA

In theory, equity returns should be neutral to inflation. In practice, however, evidence of such behavior in the short run has been difficult to come by. This literature review provides a synopsis of much of the academic and practitioner research regarding the effects of inflation on equity prices.

2016 RESEARCH FOUNDATION REVIEW PREVIEW: *FINANCIAL MARKET HISTORY* (A SUMMARY)

In 2015, the CFA Institute Research Foundation supported the Newton Centre for Endowment Asset Management in hosting the Financial Market History Workshop at the University of Cambridge Judge Business School.[1] The event, led by David Chambers and Elroy Dimson, featured many prominent speakers, including Charles D. Ellis, CFA, William Goetzmann, and Antti Ilmanen.

In 2016, the Research Foundation will release video interviews and publish a monograph featuring papers from the conference participants. Following is a summary of topics presented at the conference.

Financial Market History (a preview)

David Chambers and Elroy Dimson, co-editors

To be published 2016 by the CFA Institute Research Foundation

Preview prepared by David Chambers and Elroy Dimson

Since the 2008 financial crisis, a resurgence of interest in economic and financial history has occurred among investment professionals. The forthcoming book, titled *Financial Market History,* will discuss some of the lessons drawn from the past that may help practitioners when thinking about their portfolios. The book's editors, David Chambers and Elroy Dimson, are the academic leaders of the Newton Centre for Endowment Asset Management at the University of Cambridge in the United Kingdom.

Some investment practitioners have long understood the benefit of learning from our financial past. For example, Russell Napier, in his book *Anatomy of the Bear,* and Andrew Smithers and Stephen Wright, in their book *Valuing Wall Street,* use financial history to inform and guide their investment strategies. Many other excellent publications would repay any practitioner who wishes to gain a deeper understanding of why financial markets have developed in the manner they have over the past several hundred years. They include, to name but a few, Niall Ferguson's *The Ascent of Money,* William N. Goetzmann and K. Geert Rouwenhorst's *The Origins of Value,* Raghuram

[1]See www.jbs.cam.ac.uk/faculty-research/centres/newton-centre-for-endowment-asset-management/conferences-and-seminars/financial-market-history-workshop.

G. Rajan and Luigi Zingales's *Saving Capitalism from the Capitalists*, and William N. Goetzmann's recently published *Money Changes Everything*.

Financial Market History is an outgrowth of the Financial History Workshop that took place at the Cambridge Judge Business School in July 2015 and brings together a series of chapters from leading academics in historical finance. Their shared motivation is to examine a wide range of subjects that are particularly relevant for investors today. Collection of the essays in *Financial Market History* was supported by the CFA Institute Research Foundation, the CFA Society United Kingdom, and others.

The opening chapters deal with one of the major ways in which financial history contributes to investment practice, namely, by providing long-run series of data on various asset classes. Elroy Dimson, Paul Marsh, and Mike Staunton summarize the long-run global evidence about the risk and return characteristics of traditional asset classes, such as equities, bonds, bills, and exchange rates. Long-run return series span the broadest possible range of historical market conditions and are necessary for investors to understand likely future investment outcomes. Antti Ilmanen's essay complements this analysis by examining the time-varying properties of stocks. In particular, he considers how sensible it is to make use of long-run data series to try to time entry into and exit from markets. Finally, in this section on long-run returns, Jan Annaert, Frans Buelens, and Angelo Riva discuss some of the pitfalls to be avoided when assembling or using historical asset price data—equity and bond data in particular. The temptation to simply download historical data in modeling risk and return, without thinking about the quality of the data and the care with which return series have been compiled, is to be avoided at all costs.

Modern stock exchanges trace their origins back to Amsterdam in the early 17th century. Larry Neal's essay considers the origins and development of the most important stock market to emerge in the 19th century, the London Stock Exchange (LSE). How the LSE organized itself had implications for subsequent innovations in the way stocks were traded. Furthermore, some of the issues raised today by the emergence of electronic exchanges would have been familiar to the stock exchanges of more than a century ago. Of course, stock markets develop through companies deciding to go public. Carsten Burhop and David Chambers survey the long-run historical evidence about IPOs in the world's major stock markets. Their discussion addresses, in particular, the question of whether three phenomena—underpricing, the IPO cycle, and long-run underperformance—that are observed in modern markets existed in earlier times. Once companies have gone public, investors then care about the *liquidity* with which they can trade stocks on the exchanges. Caroline Fohlin's chapter offers a fascinating insight into how liquid the New York Stock Exchange was in the early 20th century.

Stock markets and bubble episodes are frequently mentioned in the same breath. Eugene White offers investors a survey of major bubble episodes and the most important lessons they provide for when the next bubble comes around. William Goetzmann reminds us that, although bubbles insert themselves deeply into the investor psyche, they are relatively infrequent. He examines the frequency of large, sudden run-ups in stock prices since 1900 and concludes that the chances of the market giving back its gains following a doubling in value are only about 10%. In other words, it is worth reminding ourselves that, based on the history of the 20th century, only a small fraction of stock market booms ever go sour and turn into burst bubbles. Charles Goodhart notes that financial crises usually arise when an asset bubble that has been largely financed through the expansion of bank credit turns sour. Prior to the middle of the 20th century, what led to such a crisis was often a combination of an equity bubble and bank credit expansion, but recently, the key interaction has been between housing and property booms/busts and credit expansion. Goodhart goes on to discuss the interaction between financial crises and the real economy, and he explores the potential cures for such crises that have been offered.

In addition to stocks, bonds, and bills, historians have collected data on various other assets. Olivier Accominotti discusses exchange rates and the returns to two common currency-trading strategies, namely, carry and momentum. The tendency is to think that modern currency trading began after the collapse of the Bretton Woods agreement in the 1970s, but the foreign exchange market first emerged in its modern-day form in 1919. We were largely unaware that currencies were actively traded through most of the 1920s and 1930s. Christophe Spaenjers provides investors with a fascinating insight into other assets that can be found in the portfolios of high-net-worth individuals: real estate, collectibles, and precious metals and diamonds. Much academic work has been undertaken in recent years to collect historical prices of some of these assets, and we now have a sense of their long-run performance characteristics.

Financial innovation has been an important feature of financial market development over the centuries. Geert Rouwenhorst's essay on early financial contracts is a reminder that not all innovative security designs survive and that we can learn from those that do not as well as those that do. Tom Nicholas's contribution focuses on a particularly successful innovation in the United States—that is, venture capital. He describes the origins and development of high-technology venture investing in the post-1945 period and the factors that led to its success.

Finally, we turn to what historians have concluded from studying investors themselves. The contributions from Leslie Hannah and Janette Rutterford and from Charles Ellis consider various aspects of the institutionalization of investment activity.

This book is not intended to be exhaustive. Much important work by eminent scholars has been omitted because of space limitations. Furthermore, as Barry Eichengreen's essay highlights, new frontiers in financial history are being opened up in the wake of the 2008 financial crisis. The hope of the editors is that this volume will persuade practitioners that a detailed knowledge of the past can be worthwhile in tackling the investment challenges of the future.

STANDARDS AND ADVOCACY GROUP CONTENT

The Research Foundation and the Standards and Advocacy group at CFA Institute are now partners in driving the vision of the future for investment management practitioners. As such, we are honored to provide summaries and links to some of the group's content published during 2015, including work from the Future of Finance initiative.

Addressing Financial Reporting Complexity: Investor Perspectives (January 2015)

Standard setters and regulators around the world have been working to address the issue of financial reporting complexity. So far, their efforts have focused on reduced reporting requirements to lower the compliance costs of companies. This new study gives investors, for the first time, a voice in the matter. And they have a different take on how, and why, to reduce complexity in financial reporting.

Analyzing Bank Performance: Role of Comprehensive Income (February 2015)

A source of continued debate among financial reporting stakeholders and accounting standard setters is the relevance of information reported through the "other comprehensive income" statement. To help inform the debate, this report analyzes bank data from 44 banks (in the United States, the European Union, and Canada), including many systemically important financial institutions, over an eight-year period (2006 to 2013).

Compensation Discussion and Analysis Template: Second Edition (April 2015)

The *Compensation Discussion and Analysis Template* was developed by a CFA Institute–led working group of issuers, investors, and associations to help issuers tell a story about their compensation policies, practices, and decisions and to guide issuers in creating a compensation and disclosure analysis statement that can be read and understood by average retail investors.

Shadow Banking: Policy Frameworks and Investor Perspectives on Markets-Based Finance (April 2015)

The report (which examines a diverse ecosystem spanning wholesale markets–based credit intermediation and alternative lending channels) evaluates the scope of the shadow banking system, examines policy frameworks applicable to different shadow banking entities and activities, and surveys the perspectives of investment professionals on key shadow banking issues.

European Capital Markets Union: What It Means for Investors in the EU and Globally (August 2015)

This CFA Institute white paper gives an overview of the European Commission's Capital Markets Union (CMU) initiative, including the current state of the European capital markets and what the CMU initiative could mean for investors in the European Union and globally. A CFA Institute member survey helped inform the analysis and policy considerations.

Liquidity in Equity Markets: Characteristics, Dynamics, and Implications for Market Quality (August 2015)

The report examines two practitioner concerns: (1) whether pretrade transparent (or "lit") liquidity provision is disincentivised by off-exchange trading—thus possibly increasing adverse selection risk—and (2) whether the resilience of liquidity has declined over time. Data from US, UK, and French equity markets from 2010 to 2014 provide some evidence that off-exchange trading increases the probability of adverse selection on lit venues.

An Ideal Retirement System (March 2015—Future of Finance)

This paper offers a set of retirement design principles that we hope will form the basis for debate and discussion among our members and beyond. We engaged Mercer in this project because of the growing influence of its Melbourne Mercer Global Pension Index. As the author notes, each country is at a different stage in this conversation and faces different cultural dynamics with its populace. For some readers, these principles may sound very familiar; others may consider them controversial. We are glad to share these principles as a foundation to begin a meaningful dialogue among our member network and others with interest in this subject to assess and evaluate what changes are needed in their own systems.

Environmental, Social, and Governance Issues in Investing: A Guide for Investment Professionals (October 2015—Future of Finance)

The practice of considering environmental, social, and governance (ESG) issues in investing has evolved significantly from its origins in the exclusionary screening of listed equities on the basis of moral values. A variety of methods are now being used by both value-motivated and values-motivated investors in considering ESG issues across asset classes. There is, however, a lingering misperception that the body of empirical evidence shows that ESG considerations adversely affect financial performance. For investment professionals, a key idea in the discussion of ESG issues is that systematically considering ESG issues will likely lead to more complete investment analyses and better-informed investment decisions.

Named Endowments

The CFA Institute Research Foundation acknowledges with sincere gratitude the generous contributions of the Named Endowment participants listed below.

Gifts of at least US$100,000 qualify donors for membership in the Named Endowment category, which recognizes in perpetuity the commitment toward unbiased, practitioner-oriented, relevant research that these firms and individuals have expressed through their generous support of the CFA Institute Research Foundation.

Ameritech
Anonymous
Robert D. Arnott
Theodore R. Aronson, CFA
Asahi Mutual Life
Batterymarch Financial Management
Boston Company
Boston Partners Asset Management, L.P.
Gary P. Brinson, CFA
Brinson Partners, Inc.
Capital Group International, Inc.
Concord Capital Management
Dai-Ichi Life Company
Daiwa Securities
Mr. and Mrs. Jeffrey Diermeier
Gifford Fong Associates
Investment Counsel Association of America, Inc.
Jacobs Levy Equity Management
John A. Gunn, CFA
Jon L. Hagler Foundation
Long-Term Credit Bank of Japan, Ltd.
Lynch, Jones & Ryan, LLC
Meiji Mutual Life Insurance Company
Miller Anderson & Sherrerd, LLP
John B. Neff
Nikko Securities Co., Ltd.
Nippon Life Insurance Company of Japan
Nomura Securities Co., Ltd.
Payden & Rygel
Provident National Bank
Frank K. Reilly, CFA
Salomon Brothers
Sassoon Holdings Pte. Ltd.
Scudder Stevens & Clark
Security Analysts Association of Japan
Shaw Data Securities, Inc.
Sit Investment Associates, Inc.
Standish, Ayer & Wood, Inc.
State Farm Insurance Company
Sumitomo Life America, Inc.
T. Rowe Price Associates, Inc.
Templeton Investment Counsel Inc.
Frank Trainer, CFA
Travelers Insurance Co.
USF&G Companies
Yamaichi Securities Co., Ltd.

Senior Research Fellows

Financial Services Analyst Association

For more on upcoming Research Foundation publications and webcasts, please visit www.cfainstitute.org/learning/foundation.

Research Foundation monographs are online at www.cfapubs.org.

Photo credit: Alan Barnett.

CFA Institute CEO Paul Smith, CFA (far left), talks with RF trustees Renée Blasky, CFA, and Vikram Kuriyan, CFA (left to right) before the RF 50th Anniversary Forum.

Photo credit: Alan Barnett.

Research Foundation trustee Arnie Wood (right) discusses RF board matters with past RF Chair Jeff Bailey, CFA (left).

Research Foundation trustees Diane Garnick (right) and George Hoguet, CFA (left), discuss issues during a break in the action from committee meetings.

Past RF Chair Jeff Bailey, CFA (left), observes the panel discussions with current RF Chair JT Grier, CFA (right).

RESEARCH FOUNDATION CONTRIBUTION FORM

☑ **Yes**, I want the Research Foundation to continue to fund innovative research that advances the investment management profession. Please accept my contribution* at the following level:

Thought Leadership Circle .... US$1,000,000 or more
Named Endowment .... US$100,000 to US$999,999
Research Fellow .... US$10,000 to US$99,999
Contributing Donor .... US$1,000 to US$9,999
Friend .... Up to US$999

I would like to donate US$____________________.

☐ My check is enclosed (payable to the CFA Institute Research Foundation).
☐ I would like to donate appreciated securities (send me information).
☐ Please charge my donation to my credit card.
☐ VISA ☐ MC ☐ Amex ☐ Diners

Card Number

___/___ Expiration Date

Name on card PLEASE PRINT

☐ Corporate Card
☐ Personal Card

Signature

☐ This is a pledge. Please bill me for my donation of US$ ______________
☐ I would like recognition of my donation to be:
☐ Individual donation ☐ Corporate donation ☐ Different individual

*Contibutions may be tax deductible in some countries and territories.

PLEASE PRINT NAME OR COMPANY NAME AS YOU WOULD LIKE IT TO APPEAR

PLEASE PRINT ☐ Mr. ☐ Mrs. ☐ Ms. MEMBER NUMBER ______________________

Last Name (Family Name) First (Given Name) Middle Initial

Title

Address

City State/Province Country ZIP/Postal Code

Please mail this completed form with your contribution to:
The CFA Institute Research Foundation • P.O. Box 2082
Charlottesville, VA 22902-2082 USA

For more on the CFA Institute Research Foundation, please visit www.cfainstitute.org/learning/foundation.

Made in the USA
Monee, IL
05 November 2026

67386576R00071